PROFESSIONAL ETHICS IN EDUCATION SERIES
Kenneth A. Strike, EDITOR

The Ethics of School Administration
Kenneth A. Strike, Emil J. Haller, and Jonas F. Soltis

Classroom Life as Civic Education:
Individual Achievement and Student Cooperation in Schools
David C. Bricker

The Ethics of Special Education
Kenneth R. Howe and Ofelia B. Miramontes

The Ethics of Multicultural and Bilingual Education
Barry L. Bull, Royal T. Fruehling, and Virgie Chattergy

Ethics for Professionals in Education:
Perspectives for Preparation and Practice
Kenneth A. Strike and P. Lance Ternasky, Editors

The Moral Base for Teacher Professionalism
Hugh Sockett

Ethics in School Counseling
John M. Schulte and Donald B. Cochrane

ETHICS
IN
SCHOOL COUNSELING

John M. Schulte
Donald B. Cochrane

Teachers College, Columbia University
New York and London

Published by Teachers College Press, 1234 Amsterdam Avenue, New York, NY 10027

Library of Congress Cataloging-in-Publication Data

Schulte, John M.
Ethics in school counseling / John M. Schulte and Donald Cochrane.
p. cm.—(Professional ethics in education series)
Includes bibliographical references and index.
ISBN 0-8077-3432-2 (acid-free paper)
1. Educational counseling—Moral and ethical aspects.
2. Educational counseling—Moral and ethical aspects—Case studies.
3. Student counselors—Professional ethics. 4. Student counselors—Professional ethics—Case studies. I. Cochrane, Donald B., 1940– . II. Title. III. Series.
LB1027.5.S286 1995
174'.93714—dc20 95-1544

ISBN 0-8077-3432-2 (paper)
Printed on acid-free paper
Manufactured in the United States of America
06 05 04 03 8 7 6 5 4 3 2

Contents

Preface

The fences that surround our schools do not protect our students from the many complex problems of contemporary society. The realities of social life—economic recession, changes in family structure, racial and ethnic tensions, religious controversies, gang culture, drug and alcohol abuse—influence all who attend and work in schools. School counselors are directly and personally affected by these tensions. Some in the school community may be able to concentrate on their academic or administrative specializations and remove themselves to a degree from these problems. School counselors do not have this leeway. They are assigned the task of helping students deal with the challenges of growing up and preparing for a productive and satisfying life in what some would describe as a dysfunctional culture. Difficult social and personal dilemmas come through the door of the counseling office every day.

For many years, both authors held graduate seminars for school counselors to help them grapple with ethical problems. Almost all of the students in these seminars were working in schools or similar institutions, and they brought with them some of the real problems they were confronting. The ensuing rich discussions, over the years, clarified several issues:

1. School counselors are inevitably involved in situations that generate complex ethical problems.
2. These problems are rarely amenable to simple solutions. It is not likely that a counselor can deal with these problems effectively merely by referring to laws, school board policies, or codes of ethics.
3. When faced with a complex ethical problem, the advice of others may be invaluable, but ultimately one must think one's own way through it.
4. Thinking through ethical problems is not easy. To do so effectively, one needs

- an understanding of what makes a problem an *ethical* problem;
- a set of clear concepts relevant to ethical thinking;
- an understanding of what is involved in an ethical analysis;
- considerable practice in analyzing ethical problems related to school counseling.

Many training programs designed to prepare counselors for their work reduce the ethical dimension of the profession to knowledge of a code of ethics. However helpful codes may be, the moral life is too complex to be so neatly encapsulated. Analogously, the Ten Commandments may provide a solid basis for an ethical life, but we face many ethical dilemmas about which the commandments are either silent, ambiguous, or—possibly—offer contradictory advice. Given that counseling is fraught with ethical problems, the interesting question is why psychology and, in particular, counseling strives to circumvent this aspect of experience.

Perhaps counseling still labors under a Freudian legacy (though most other aspects of this school of thought may have been jettisoned) in which values are seen as products of the superego and, thus, are essentially irrational. In addition, deeply held values are often seen as the source of "psychological problems." This view, stated so starkly, must be rejected. The source of a value should not be confused with its validity. Some early childhood experience may be deeply lodged in my unconscious and may "cause" me to promote justice in all of my activities or recoil in horror at a report of child abuse, but my autobiography is irrelevant to the soundness of these values.

Moral principles can be justified apart from any psychological account of causation (Peters, 1960). Further, not all feelings of, say, guilt are irrational or amoral, however severe the symptoms. A client may be completely paralyzed, yet the proper treatment may be to have him or her face the moral situation that gave rise to the feelings. To remove the guilt feelings cosmetically (some might say "psychologically") would be a serious disservice to the client (Buber, 1957). So, although values may be the cause of some psychological problems, at times it is the values that must be respected and not be altered. To know when to respect, maintain, and validate a client's values requires considerable ethical discrimination. At other times—say, when the values that are causing stress are sexist, racist, or exploitive—it is completely appropriate to question the client's values. That is, a counselor has on occasion the responsibility to be a moral educator.

In the mid-1960s, counselors discovered that the profession had, at times, been used to maintain mainstream (and often sexist and racist) values. Counselors were accused of purporting to promote mental health while acting as agents of a corporate and oppressive elite by imposing the values implicit in their counseling theories on unsuspecting clients. A new generation of counselors branded all value judgments as "judgmental" and sought to facilitate a process in which clients discovered their own values in a process of self-realization. This pendulum swing against excessive and deceptive paternalism resulted in an irresponsible and equally deceptive moral license. Clarifying which values are either personally or culturally relative and morally acceptable in a pluralistic society, and which are so fundamental that they are not morally optional, has always been a major goal of moral philosophy. In this book, we stake out such a distinction.

Chapter 1 begins with the analysis of concepts that are vital to ethical thinking. School counselors inevitably are required to make value judgments, and so, we attempt to clarify the notions of "value" and "judgment." Chapter 2 introduces "value orientations" and demonstrates how influential they may be in counseling. Chapter 3 focuses on a particular kind of values—namely, ethical values. We offer a brief introduction to the field of ethics and discuss what is involved in ethical problems and making ethical judgments.

The next two chapters are devoted to a discussion of ethical reasoning. Chapter 4 introduces the basic elements of the ethical point of view and strategies for engaging in ethical reasoning, and Chapter 5 provides a more detailed exploration of the application of moral principles to counseling situations.

Chapter 6 examines the types of ethical problems that occur very frequently in the professional lives of school counselors. A detailed analysis of one case follows in Chapter 7. Chapter 8 consists of a compilation of typical counseling cases for readers to wrestle with. Finally, Chapter 9 discusses the needs of counselors, in light of the ethical dimensions of their work, and the responsibilities of the profession to its members.

Acknowledgments

This book is dedicated to the hundreds of counselors who, for more than two decades, challenged our ethical theory with examples from their professional experience. We hope, in turn, that our theory—tested and refined—will illuminate future practice.

Nancy Cochrane deserves credit for clearing away the underbrush of our prose and allowing our ideas to enter the light of day.

Stanton Teal's constructive criticism of early drafts assisted us greatly.

Carol Collins, our editor at Teachers College Press, warrants special thanks for her unfailing patience and encouragement.

We are grateful to Betty Lembke for contributing her secretarial expertise to the project.

We are indebted to the Publications Fund at the University of Saskatchewan for its timely assistance in bringing this project to completion.

We can now return to our families. We have been gone a long time.

CHAPTER 1

Value Judgments: The Case of Maria

Things are humming along for Ms. Larkin, a first-year guidance counselor at Riverside High. Her routine and relatively simple duties, such as assisting students with their class schedules, administering various tests, and providing career information, have been interspersed with problems of a more personal nature, generally arising from the normal processes of adolescence. She has developed a good relationship with faculty and students and feels she has worked efficiently and well.

Her first appointment today is with a 10th-grade student named Maria. Until recently, Maria has been a good student, full of enthusiasm and school spirit. But lately, she has become listless and depressed. Several of Maria's teachers have noted her lack of involvement in classroom discussions and a sharp decline in the quality of her work. Because of these changes, her homeroom teacher has referred her to Ms. Larkin.

Through tears, Maria reveals she is pregnant and very uncertain about her boyfriend's commitment to their relationship. She has not told him for fear of losing him, nor her parents for fear of their reaction. Her parents take their religion, which prohibits premarital sex, very seriously, so she doubts they will be sympathetic or supportive. She describes her father's temper as violent. She is unwilling to reveal the identity of her boyfriend and begs Ms. Larkin not to contact her parents. She also mentions how much she would like to remain in school and graduate with her classmates.

When Maria finishes explaining the situation, she turns toward the counselor with a sorrowful, pleading look. She does not know what to do and is depending on Ms. Larkin to give her some direction.

* * *

How school counselors face such serious human predicaments profoundly affects many lives. Although some cases may be quite straightforward, others will have unique features that defy handling in routine ways. No matter how thoroughly professionals have been prepared, they will encounter problems for which there are no easy answers. Counseling theories, job descriptions, school policies, and professional codes of ethics may furnish some guidelines, but sooner or later, a situation arises like the one Ms. Larkin is facing. The counselor must navigate uncharted waters. Yet, no one is better poised to make crucial decisions. Ms. Larkin's effectiveness in this situation depends on her ability to think her way through the problem with little or no outside help.

At such times, it is necessary to use ethical reasoning. Such reasoning, to be effective, demands the understanding and training of its practitioner—in this case, the school counselor. The opportunity for practice in a variety of hypothetical cases is useful for the counselor to have before he or she begins working with real students in school settings.

MAKING VALUE JUDGMENTS

In deciding on the soundest course of action, Ms. Larkin faces the overarching difficulty of how to help Maria with her problems. To do this, she must make a series of value judgments. Several questions are likely to confront her:

1. Am I the appropriate agent to help Maria? Would it be a good idea to refer her to someone else or to consult another professional about this case?
2. Should I comply with Maria's request not to tell her parents about the situation? Should I try to convince Maria that she badly needs the support system her family might be able to provide?
3. Should I take any steps to locate Maria's boyfriend?
4. Is Maria mature and emotionally stable enough to deliberate rationally about her situation and arrive at a sound judgment about what to do? If so, is my role simply to lay out a series of alternatives and allow Maria to choose? If not, should I encourage, or even prescribe, one course of action?
5. Should I dismiss Maria at the end of her appointment and stick to my busy schedule, or is her situation serious enough to warrant my canceling other appointments in order to confer with her further?
6. What, if anything, should I tell the homeroom teacher and other staff members who are concerned about Maria?

Each of these questions calls for a value judgment. Similar questions may arise in other types of school counseling sessions. Clarifying what is involved in a "value judgment" requires examining briefly its two components—"value" and "judgment."

Judgment

Green (1960) points out that "judging" can involve ranking or grading, as in the case of a judge rating a show dog. It can involve estimating, as when one judges how long a trip will take. It can also involve predicting, as when a politician judges the likely reactions of his or her constituents to a proposed bill. To clarify its relation to other concepts, Green concocts a little scenario.

Imagine three people competing in a contest at a county fair. Contestants are asked to estimate the number of beans in a large jar. The first contestant, Lydia, is an extremely busy woman. She supports the charity that is sponsoring the contest but has no time to attend the fair. She has no information about the size of the jar or the kind of beans that are inside. She simply selects numbers she thinks are lucky and mails in her contest form. Darren, the second contestant, is greedy and has no scruples. In the middle of the night, he secretly enters the room where the jar is kept, empties the contents, and carefully counts the beans. Then he returns the beans to the jar and places it on the shelf. The next day, he submits his entry. Carolyn, the third contestant, puts her mathematical prowess to good use. She estimates the volume of the jar in cubic inches and the number of beans it would take to fill a cubic inch. She multiplies and arrives at a figure which she submits as her entry.

Green points out that it would be odd to describe what Lydia and Darren did as "judging." Lydia's reasons for choosing the number she submitted had no logical connection to estimating the number of beans in the jar. It is more accurate to portray what she did as merely "guessing" or "imagining." It would also seem strange to depict Darren's response as judging. He did not have to calculate the number of beans because he knew it already. It is only Carolyn who could reasonably be said to be judging.

Green uses this scenario to arrive at a continuum representing different degrees of certitude:

Guessing ◄——► Judging ◄——► Knowing

For someone's choice to be a judgment, it must be based on reasons, rules, or principles. If there is no basis at all for the choice, or if the reasons for it are not connected in some logical way, then it was a guess, not a judgment. On the other hand, if something is absolutely certain, it is knowledge and does not require judgment.

The continuum suggests that the concept of judging has broad application. Sometimes a judgment is just a little better than a guess, or it may be practically certain knowledge. The borders between judging and the other two concepts blur at points.

Judging is central to much of our moral life. When deciding what we ought to do, we must bring relevant principles to bear on what we refer to loosely as the "facts of the case." Though the moral life does possess a few certainties (for example, rape is always wrong), much of the time we live in varying degrees of quandary. On these occasions, we must rely on judgment. This is certainly true for counselors.

Value

To say that something has value is to ascribe to it a certain worth or merit. The words "good" and "bad" are often used to indicate that something has positive or negative value, such as a reference to a good school or a bad poker player. However, when people describe something as good—say a movie or a meal—they are not necessarily saying anything more about it than that it gives them pleasure or satisfaction. When a statement like "This is good" means no more than "I like this," nothing is suggested about the worth or merit of the object. The speaker is merely conveying a personal preference. This statement could not be incorrect unless, of course, it is a lie.

It is very important to distinguish statements about what people like and dislike from value claims. If someone says, "I like that automobile," some information is being disclosed about that person that is probably only of interest to the salesperson who is trying to sell the car. This is stating a personal affinity. If the salesperson says, "This is a really fine automobile," a claim is being made about the car and not about the salesperson. A value claim is being made. An individual may have no idea why he or she likes the car, or care, but the salesperson will be expected to provide good reasons to justify the claim that the car is a good one.

It is certainly true that many things that are recognized as having great value are also things that people tend to like—things like security, friendship, health, peace of mind, and leisure time, to name a few. However, likes and dislikes are not reliable indicators of value. Many people like to use tobacco and alcohol to relax, though these substances are harmful. Many people intensely dislike going to the dentist, but that does not mean that it is a bad thing to do. To determine the value of something, there is no alternative to assessing its worth.

Selecting standards. A simple example is needed to grasp what is involved in assessing the worth of something. If while trying to slice a loaf of bread a person succeeds only in reducing it to a flattened mess of crumbs, he or she is likely to say, "This is a terrible breadknife." This is ascribing negative value to the breadknife, based on the assumption that breadknives can be judged by standards, and that this knife does not meet them. What makes this value assessment relatively simple is the fact that there are clear and commonly accepted standards for judging the value of a breadknife.

Our car shopping scenario provides a slightly more complex example of value assessment. When asked about the value of the car, the salesperson may rhapsodize about the car's beauty, power, and comfort. But suppose the customer is most interested in selecting a car that is safe, reliable, and economical. Apparently, they are judging the value of the car by different standards or, at least, a different hierarchy of standards. People often disagree about the appropriate standards to apply when assessing the value of something. This leads some to the dangerous conclusion that values are merely matters of personal taste. Some people enjoy opera; others do not. Some people like to spend their vacations in the mountains; others prefer the seashore.

It is certainly true that many choices are merely matters of personal taste, and also that reasonable people can select different standards in assessing the value of something. But these facts do not lead to the conclusion that in every circumstance just any set of standards will do. Reasonable people may have good personal reasons for using particular standards in making a value assessment. For example, a person with a large family might use the size of the interior as a standard in shopping for a car. Reasonable people may also argue about the relative importance of such factors as safety, reliability, power, and economy and come to different conclusions. However, one could select standards for an assessment that are much less reasonable, such as the amount of chrome on a car or the number of buttons on the panel. Selecting standards of value is, indeed, a matter of opinion, but not all opinions are equally reasonable.

Although selecting appropriate standards for a value assessment is more complex in a situation like shopping for a car than in selecting a breadknife, it is an infinitely simpler task than the one that faces Ms. Larkin in deciding how to respond to Maria's situation. We will consider this later when we return to the case of Maria. What is important to recognize here is the critical role that selecting standards plays in making judgments.

Using Information

The soundness of a value assessment often depends on the accuracy of relevant information. Suppose a couple selects a new car on the basis of the salesperson's testimony that this particular model has the combination of reliability, comfort, and economy they are looking for. They value the car highly because they believe it meets the standards they have established. If the salesperson's claims about the car are false, their assessment is unsound.

To judge which of various alternatives is the most desirable, accurate information is crucial. How should money be invested? Should more workers be hired for a business? Should an individual quit one job to seek another? Questions like these call for judgments, and it would be wise to gather as much relevant information as possible before making a value assessment. However, it is important to note that information alone can never establish what it is good or bad to do. When considering two employment opportunities, one gathers facts about salary, fringe benefits, working conditions, possibilities for advancement, and so on, but appropriate standards must be determined before one can assess the significance of these facts.

VALUE JUDGMENTS IN THE CASE OF MARIA

Value judgments occur in situations in which people try to decide the merits of something or the right course of action to take. They are not based on absolute certainty, or impulse, or whim. The person who makes them lacks certainty regarding what is good and must come to a decision on the basis of relevant reasons and evidence. The more substantial the reasons and the more compelling the evidence, the more grounded the appraisal.

Thus, making a value judgment entails applying certain standards, and this task can be simple or complex. Many of the judgments that school counselors are called on to make are complex. Acquiring accurate information is often an essential piece of the puzzle.

Different kinds of standards are relevant for determining the most desirable response to a client, and they may not be compatible. We can see this by considering the various alternatives open to Ms. Larkin in responding to Maria. She could focus exclusively on Maria's well-being.

Her overriding concern would be what she could do to decrease Maria's anguish and increase her chances for a happy, productive life. She would then make all decisions on this basis. She could decide that she must include well-established community standards in making her assessment. Ms. Larkin must consider relevant laws, school board policies, and the widely held conviction that parents have the primary responsibility for raising children and dealing with their problems. She could decide that her own value orientation must inform her judgment.

Maria's dilemma illustrates that standards from these three sources will not be compatible. Most counselors will have some strong convictions about the right of a woman to control what happens to her own body and at what point a human embryo becomes a person and acquires rights that others must respect. Ms. Larkin might well decide that ignoring her own deeply held convictions about these things would be a violation of personal integrity. Human lives are likely to be significantly affected by counselors' judgments and actions. And the stakes are much higher when one is determining how to respond to a client like Maria than they are when choosing a car or a breadknife.

A counselor's judgment is based on a prediction that an action will result in desirable consequences. However, the effects of one's actions on others are notoriously difficult to predict. Ms. Larkin may decide to call, or not call, Maria's parents on the basis of her best predictions about their reaction, but whatever her assessment of the situation, it is quite possible that it will be inaccurate no matter how carefully she makes it.

In a given case, several persons are likely to make their own value judgments about what the counselor should do. In Ms. Larkin's situation, Maria has indicated some general directions she thinks the counselor should take, and Maria's parents, no doubt, would have their own views. The principal and teachers of the school, as well as Ms. Larkin's colleagues in the counseling office, might have strong opinions about the best course of action. Ms. Larkin may well find that her judgments are in conflict with the judgments of others who are involved. It would be arrogant of her to ignore them on the assumption that their judgments could not possibly be better than her own. On the other hand, she could not simply allow the judgments of others to prevail, for that would be to abdicate the responsibility of her profession.

Ms. Larkin must make one important decision on the way to a final resolution: she has to decide whether or not to contact Maria's parents. The first thing to note is that this determination meets the requirements for a value judgment. She must decide if this action would help or harm Maria and the others involved. It is unlikely that Ms. Larkin (or anyone else) would think she *knows* the answer to this question and, thus, has no need to deliberate. It would be irrational for her to reach a decision in some arbitrary way, like flipping a coin. If she comes to a decision by examining her options, then whatever the decision, it is a value judgment.

As stated earlier, value judgments are made on the basis of value standards. Ms. Larkin might begin her task by identifying standards that are both sound and relevant to the problem. Her first rough formulation of a standard might be, "I should do whatever is most likely to help Maria," or "I should avoid doing things that are likely to harm Maria." Either formulation would lead directly to the need for determining the likely effect for Maria of contacting her parents. As Ms. Larkin grapples with this problem, there are several questions to ponder:

1. From her training and experience, she knows that adolescents need a support system, especially at critical times. Are there others besides Maria's family who could provide this support for Maria?
2. Maria thinks her parents would react negatively to the news that she is pregnant. Should Ms. Larkin assume that she is right about this or try to secure more information and make her own judgment?
3. If she decides to contact Maria's parents, it seems likely that Maria will feel resentful and hurt, and that their relationship may be weakened or destroyed. Is the chance of obtaining the support of her parents worth this risk?
4. Is the fact that Maria does not want Ms. Larkin to contact her parents a sufficient reason for not doing so?

These questions indicate that Ms. Larkin lacks vital information. School counselors rarely have available all of the information they would want in deciding how to respond to a client with a serious problem. In addition, the information they have is not always reliable. We cannot expect omniscience of Ms. Larkin, but rather, sound judgments based on what she is able to learn about the situation.

Note that the last question is different from the others. It does not conjecture about possible actions and consequences. Ms. Larkin is considering whether she is obligated to respect Maria's position regarding contact with her parents. This question may lead Ms. Larkin to reconsider her rough formulation of a value standard on which to base her judgment. At the outset, her considerations were limited to what might be helpful or harmful to Maria in terms of her physical, emotional, and social well-being. The fourth question is a different sort of ethical question. Are there some circumstances in which it is right for the counselor to overrule the expressed wishes of the client? This question might lead Ms. Larkin to recognize that ethical standards must be considered when a counselor is trying to establish what would be helpful and harmful to clients. (Ethical standards and how they apply to value judgments are discussed in Chapter 3.)

At some point, Ms. Larkin's thinking is likely to go beyond consideration of Maria's well-being. Questions like these are likely to arise:

1. Is there anything mandated by law or school board policy regarding sharing information with parents about their children?
2. Do I have any ethical obligations towards Maria's parents in this situation?

Ms. Larkin realizes that in arriving at a value judgment she must consider standards other than those that pertain exclusively to Maria. Her questions also point to a number of very serious ethical problems. What obligations do counselors have to others when working with a client? Is a counselor ever justified in breaking laws or school board policies to help a client?

We have identified only some of the questions Ms. Larkin might reflect on and the problems that might develop as a result of her deliberations. However, it is already apparent that much is involved in reaching a value judgment in a complex situation. As we have seen, thinking a way through to a value judgment is not likely to be a straightforward, linear process. Attempts to answer initial questions lead to others. Nonetheless, we can identify in a general way the steps Ms. Larkin should take in deciding whether or not to contact Maria's parents:

1. She should identify the value standards upon which to base her judgment. If these standards conflict, she should determine which takes priority.
2. She should carefully consider the probable consequences of informing Maria's parents and of not doing so. At this stage, she may recognize gaps in her knowledge of the situation. For example, how are the parents likely to respond if she tells them? Is this step mandated by law or school board policy? She should do her best to acquire all pertinent information.
3. She should evaluate the likely results on the basis of the value standards she has identified as relevant to the situation.

Deciding whether or not to inform Maria's parents is only one of many value judgments Ms. Larkin will have to make. For example, suppose she decides that it would be a good idea to contact them. She must still decide how to do it. Should she simply call them in and tell them that their daughter is expecting? Should she try to persuade Maria to tell them? Should she contact Maria's mother and solicit her aid in dealing with Maria's father? Deciding *how* to notify Maria's parents would require Ms. Larkin to deliberate in a manner parallel to the way in which she would reach her decision to inform them.

SUMMARY

A value statement is a claim that something has worth or merit. A personal preference statement, such as "I like this," is not a value claim. However, a person's choice of words is not always reliable for distinguishing between the two. We may have to ask a few questions to find out if there is a normative basis for a statement.

A judgment involves estimating, ranking, or rating something. Sometimes it requires making predictions. Unlike guessing or knowing, judgments are made in situations where reasons and evidence exist but are insufficient for us to be certain about what is true or right. The better the arguments and the more compelling the evidence the more credible the judgment.

A value judgment involves formulating standards by which to evaluate a situation. This tends to be a complex task. Although facts are important in making such assessments, facts alone cannot establish whether something is good or bad. Reasonable persons can come to conflicting assessments, but this does not mean that value judgments are merely preferences or that one view is as sound as another.

CHAPTER 2

Value Orientations: The Cases of Angela and Janek

Every art and every inquiry, and similarly every action and pursuit, is thought to aim at some good. . . .

—*Aristotle,* The Politics

Ms. Hahn, a counselor at Smith Regional High School, has set aside the afternoon to meet with parents. Her first appointment is with Ms. Chianti, who is concerned about the effects of the school program on her daughter, Angela. From several conversations with Angela, Ms. Hahn has the impression that the student is an academically strong, well-adjusted 10th grader. That is why she is surprised when Ms. Chianti tells her that she and her husband are considering transferring Angela from public school to a nearby parochial school. Ms. Chianti adds quickly that they are hesitant to remove Angela because they like many things about the school. Angela is making good progress academically and seems psychologically and socially at ease in the school. She has confidence in herself, likes her teachers, and has developed close friendships with many of her classmates.

What is troubling the Chiantis is the moral and spiritual development of their daughter. They see religion as the foundation of a good life and believe that it establishes our most important goals and provides unerring guidelines in human affairs. It is their conviction that the basis of our ethical obligations is revealed in the Word of God. The Chiantis do not see the public school as an evil place, nor school personnel as the devil's agents. They recognize that a public institution in this society must serve the needs of people of many religious denominations and ethnic groups and, therefore, cannot provide for the different spiritual and moral needs of everyone.

When Angela reached school age, they would have preferred to send her to a parochial school but lacked the financial resources. They thought they would be able to provide for her spiritual and moral development themselves with the help of the weekend classes and youth programs at their church. However, things are not working out as they had wished. Although little in the formal curriculum at the public school troubles them, they are very concerned about the more subtle influences of daily school life on their daughter: Angela seems to be learning that being just like every other child in her group and getting along well with them are the most important things in the world. She wants to dress, talk, and act just like her friends do, and the Chiantis find many of the prevailing attitudes and practices of the children unacceptable.

After hearing about the fun-filled weekends of her friends, Angela is beginning to express unwillingness to attend religious instruction at the church. Freedom, independence, and individual resourcefulness are fostered in the school environment. The Chiantis are not entirely opposed to these values, but they note that Angela seems to be learning that life goals and lifestyles are entirely matters of personal choice—that one should be able to be and do just about anything one wants so long as no one gets hurt. They are concerned that Angela will fail to acquire their deeply held conviction that God's plan for a person's life takes precedence over an individual's personal desires. They believe, for example, that men and women are equal but are given different roles to play. Heading a family, protecting it, and earning the money to support it is primarily a man's role. It is not wrong for a woman to work too, so long as her job does not detract from her most important role, that of loving wife and nurturing mother.

In spite of these concerns, the Chiantis are reluctant to remove Angela from public school. Not only would it be a serious financial hardship to do so, but, perhaps even more important, they know that Angela is likely to be upset by the move. They are worried that forcing her to leave her friends and a school program she finds very exciting and rewarding could lead her to rebel. They recognize that the move might have effects opposite to those they desire. Angela's resistance to the values they think are essential to a good life could be increased rather than decreased. Ms. Chianti wants the school counselor to assist her and her husband in making the right decision for the long-term welfare and happiness of their daughter.

Ms. Hahn is somewhat taken aback by Ms. Chianti's concern. Angela's cumulative record indicates that she is thriving in the school environment—at least given the norm. From all reports, she is a happy, outgoing girl, a good student, and an active participant in a wide variety of school activities. Ms. Hahn gives her full and empathetic attention as Ms. Chianti spells out her concerns, but inwardly she cannot help but wonder why parents like the Chiantis seem so intent on disrupting what she sees as the natural development of a happy child into a productive and fulfilled adult.

Ms. Hahn's value orientation is quite different from Ms. Chianti's. Her parents encouraged independent thought and judgment from the time she was very young. Religion was not an important part of her family life. During adolescence, she took a passing interest in religion that her parents neither encouraged nor discouraged. She attended the services of a variety of denominations for a few months but found them unsatisfying. She thought that the concerns of some of the churches she attended were too remote from the important problems of living. Other churches took a more direct interest in social affairs, but she resented the dogmatic pronouncements they made about how people should live their lives.

Ms. Hahn believes that fostering independence and personal resourcefulness are among the most important things schools can do. She thinks it is their obligation to teach the value of freedom and to encourage students at all levels to establish their own life goals. She thinks that, in spite of their good intentions, some parents do a disservice to their children by imposing on them their own religious beliefs.

It is clear that Ms. Chianti and Ms. Hahn see Angela's situation quite differently. To Ms. Chianti, the problem is a school atmosphere that is fostering values that are harmful to the spiritual and moral development of her daughter. As a trained professional, Ms. Hahn will resist the urge to make a snap judgment about the nature of the problem, but her first impression is that Angela has been doing just fine and would continue to do so if her parents would allow it. Their well-meaning but overprotective attitudes are likely to do more harm than good.

* * *

Ms. Hahn hardly has time to file the Chianti papers before Mr. Dufek arrives for his appointment. He is considering home schooling his son, Janek, but wants to discuss the issue with a counselor before making a final decision. Though starting from a position very different from the Chiantis', the Dufeks are also concerned about the moral and spiritual growth of their child. Although they have no religious beliefs to speak of, they have a strong sense of what the school should be doing to promote authenticity, moral sensitivity, interpersonal skills, and a commitment to equality.

Paradoxically, in contrast to the Chiantis, they do see the school as an evil place. The Dufeks' litany is long. Janek has been learning from his peers that personality is more important than character, that relationships are not morally serious matters, and that inclusion in the in-group is very desirable, although the cost in personal integrity might be high. Despite policy declarations to the contrary, the Dufeks believe that schools teach sexist attitudes. The school is large, bureaucratic, and impersonal. The curriculum has been drained of human substance: Matters of family life, sexuality, morality, and religion are deemed too controversial to be discussed. The literature in English classes is trivial, music is reduced to musicals, and art simply does not exist at the school. Teachers' rhetoric about emancipating students is a cruel joke. In the midst of all the school's banality, diversion, and conformity, the Dufeks believe that Janek is losing the capacity to speak "with his own voice."

The source of the Chiantis' disenchantment is derived from their religious roots outside of the school, whereas the Dufeks' dissatisfaction arises from within by taking the school's own declared goals at face value. They had been led to believe that schools taught, among other things, moral reflection, critical thinking, "healthy lifestyles," and cultural and civic values. The Dufeks do not see the school as having either the vision or the courage to promote these goals.

* * *

Ms. Hahn is distressed by this second onslaught of the afternoon. As with Angela, she had always seen Janek as successful in school. He had scored high marks, been active in extracurricular activities, and had many friends. She could hardly have expected to be faced with these two cases. Now she has to defend the school (if that is her role) against criticism from both the secular left and the religious right. Frankly, she was never prepared for these sorts of challenges. "What program," she muses, "prepares counselors to consider critically the structure of schools and the curriculum? Certainly not mine."

She begins to doubt her easygoing liberalism. She has always had faith in public institutions of which one of the most important is the public school. She is generally optimistic about the future and has faith in human progress. She believes that differences can always be reconciled (wasn't that a fundamental belief in counseling theory?) if only people would use their capacity to reason rather than exaggerate their differences. Now all of the assumptions are under pressure.

VALUE SYSTEMS UNDERLYING CONVICTIONS

The cases of Angela and Janek illustrate that both school counselors and clients bring value orientations with them to their counseling sessions.

Although it may be impossible to provide a precise definition of a value orientation, it might be satisfactory to describe it as a framework of beliefs, perhaps not fully developed or internally consistent, about such fundamental matters as God, good and evil, human nature, society and culture, and conceptions of and conditions for the "good life."

Because value orientations affect how we see the world, they influence the beliefs we hold in particular situations about what is good and bad, right and wrong. In our daily experience, we speak about concrete decisions stemming from these basic beliefs. For example, someone who believes that males and females have fundamentally different natures, and so markedly divergent life scripts, will advocate that different but appropriate schooling should be provided for boys and girls. (Rousseau's classic statement of this position in *Emile* (1974) remains worthy of careful consideration, alongside Wollstonecraft's *A vindication of the rights of woman* (1891).)

Everyone with a modicum of maturity and psychological adjustment has a value orientation. Although many individuals may not be fully aware of its contents, virtually everyone has some strong convictions of this sort. Discussions that involve these basic commitments are often volatile because they are closely connected to one's sense of identity; to be critical of the value orientations of others is often seen as tantamount to attacking their sense of self. The beliefs that comprise someone's value orientation may not be entirely consistent. For example, one may be a "let-the-buyer-beware" merchant during the week and a "love-thy-neighbor" Christian at Sunday services. Often individuals become aware of some basic value assumptions as a result of a serious personal problem, like a life-threatening illness, or by considering important social issues like abortion or the rights of homosexuals. But the conditions under which self-knowledge is gained need not be this dramatic, as Ms. Hahn is learning.

Many influences contribute to the formation and modification of a person's value orientation. Children acquire beliefs from their parents—whether they are taught intentionally or not. Value orientation is also influenced by school experiences at all levels. Family life, work experiences, religion, media, and peer groups all make a contribution.

The Counselor

School counselors, like everyone else, are subject to these influences and have a value orientation when they begin their professional training. Despite disclaimers by some in the field, counseling theories themselves possess value orientations, and, thus, to subscribe to a particular theory is to accept its underlying view of how the world is and what it might (or should) become. Counseling theories incorporate a view about what is possible, practical, and desirable to promote. Clients are to adopt this perspective and, with it, a certain assessment of the world: what it should offer, what it is reasonable to expect from others, and who, in the midst of all this, one should strive to become.

Current counseling practices, for example, promote "end-states," such as self-realization, self-actualization, personality integration, maturity, autonomy, adjustment, and rationality. Given the logic of counseling theories, even diagnoses are not value-neutral: To judge that someone needs counseling is to hold that they are deficient in some way and can be helped by counseling techniques. The resistance of clients to treatment might be evidence that they are really in need of attention, or it could mean that they are objecting to the values that underlie the theory. It is important for the counselor to be able to distinguish between these two types of opposition, for they need to be handled quite differently. The advisor needs to recognize that counseling theories are meant to be practical and aim at some good. Failure in this regard results in "covert values imperialism"—that is, a particular values orientation being imposed on the client under the guise of a value-neutral theory. The beginning of wisdom for the counselor is to understand the values imbedded in such theories and to subject them to thorough critical analysis.

Some counselors may mistakenly think it possible and desirable to maintain value neutrality when working with clients, but in reality this is logically impossible, since every counselor has in mind a scheme, whether well-examined or not, which maps positive directions in which a client should move. To have no such scheme would be morally indefensible, since it means the counselor has no way to monitor whether a client is progressing or regressing. If value neutrality were possible, no counselor would ever be justified in taking any action to deter a child from running away or a sex offender from molesting a child.

Try to imagine a counselor without any strong beliefs about human purposes, well-being, or how people should treat each other, both in general and in specific relationships, like husband to wife, parent to child, and counselor to client. Try to imagine a school counselor who had no idea about human capacities, student progress, or child and adolescent development, and further, no conception of moral goodness. Without question, a counselor must have these kinds of understanding, but also a view about how they are to be employed. About that, there can be much heated but reasonable debate. Given that this value dimension must exist in counseling, clashes between the value orientation of the client and that of the counselor will take place from time to time. The counselor's value orientation will be both personal and professional in origin.

The Client

From the description of the case, we see a glimmer of Ms. Chianti's value orientation. We learn that, for her, the only source of reliable knowledge about good and evil, human nature, and the ultimate purposes for human life is the revealed Word of God. We learn that she believes that the most important role for a woman is that of nurturing wife and mother and that social acceptance and approval are not very important values. Her dissatisfaction with the public school and her belief that Angela would probably receive a better education in parochial school stem from these basic beliefs.

Mr. Dufek, on the other hand, draws his basic values from secular notions of authenticity and naturalness. Although his views on gender issues differ sharply from Ms. Chianti's, they are both critical of the pressure on their children to conform to peer standards: Angela should remain true to her God, and Janek should actualize his real self. Both parents believe that the public school atmosphere promotes, or at least tolerates, artificial values and superficial relationships.

The School

The case studies reveal another source of possible conflict surrounding value orientations. Ms. Chianti expresses concern about some of the values like freedom and individual resourcefulness that the school is intentionally fostering, whereas Mr. Dufek is complaining that the school places far too little emphasis on these goals. Although they make different judgments about the importance or the appropriateness of these aims, they both apparently realize that a school has a value orientation of its own and that some aspects of the value orientation of Angela's and Janek's school are incompatible with their own.

Some values, like honesty and concern for others, are often taught intentionally. Others may be a function of what is often described as "the hidden curriculum." Through symbolic gestures and budget appropriations, schools signal to students the relative importance of sports in relation to academic achievements. Despite official rhetoric about the value of cooperation and open inquiry, students may learn that it is wrong to help a classmate who is having difficulty with an assignment or to question the claims teachers make in class. Whether clearly identified or not, a school's operating practices, if not its policies, will reflect an underlying orientation about how children should be treated and how staff members should interact. Students learn quickly who has the power to make and execute decisions and who (if anyone) has the right to question, appeal, or reverse them.

When Values Differ

Counselors, with their value orientations, enter schools that have their own priorities and consequently counselors may find themselves bumping up against schools' political realities. Let us suppose that Ms. Larkin's principal had let it be known that he would not tolerate any controversy. Although she might think that counseling Maria to obtain an abortion might be in the student's best interests, she also knows that, should her role become public, her own position would be jeopardized. Imagine that in Ms. Hahn' s school, the size of the school budget depends on enrollments. The principal has encouraged counselors to do all they can to keep students in school. Counselors may find themselves in political predicaments: Ms. Hahn may feel that if the Chiantis and Dufeks withdraw their children, it will reflect badly on her. School priorities can have a chilling effect on good counseling.

We have made much of clashes between value orientations because they are generally underemphasized in the literature. But it is not inevitable that differences in value orientation will generate an ethical problem for the counselor. Imagine a counselor who believes that students, in general, are better off if their parents divorce rather than fight all the time. In most instances, this belief is unlikely to cause ethical problems. Even if it were not difficult to establish whether divorce would benefit a child, it is, more often than not, a matter outside of the school counselor's area of responsibility.

Differences of value orientation among those who live and work in the school community are probably inevitable unless the school has been established on the basis of a particular value orientation. Experienced school counselors are likely to encounter many situations in which their value orientations are quite different from those of their coworkers. In most of these situations, the differences and similarities are probably too remote from the problems at hand to cause any serious ethical friction or provide enough common ground for all concerned to address a problem in a productive manner.

For example, both a set of parents and the school counselor may be considering ways to improve a student's study habits or to deter a student's disruptive classroom behavior. There may be some differences in value orientation between parents and counselor, but the differences may be irrelevant to the problem they are addressing, or they may not be serious enough to prevent them from arriving at decisions that genuinely help the student. Similarly, the differences between the view of the school counselor and a teacher regarding the sanctity of a marriage contract may not prevent them from working together to help a child whose parents are going through a divorce. In many situations, a difference of value orientation between counselor and client, or counselor and teacher, may be helpful in enabling those involved to see a situation from different perspectives.

It is also important for counselors to recognize that their role in a school has both professional and practical limits. It is not their job to solve every problem and right every wrong. From their perspective, many conditions in the school and community may be harmful to the welfare of students, parents, and fellow educators. For example, they may know that many of their students endure conditions of squalor at home. As professional educators or members of the community, counselors may feel obliged to join others to fight against injustice and improve living conditions. As counselors, however, they have limited responsibility and power to effect change. Thus, they need not feel guilt (as distinct from regret) at not being able to bring the New Jerusalem to their community.

To some extent, then, counselors have to take their cases as they come and work within narrow parameters. However, in many cases, part of the therapy might involve the radicalization of students, that is, awakening in them the sense that, individually and collectively, much can be done to effect change both in the school and the community. Part of the counseling responsibility may be to contribute to the moral education of clients, not just by encouraging them to desist from antisocial behavior but by pointing the way to constructive alternatives. The counselor ought not to be naive about the ramifications of such initiatives. Political emancipation is fraught with risks, for often the appropriate action challenges "powers that be." But then, no one ever claimed that the moral life would be comfortable, and the activist counselor's never will be.

ETHICAL DILEMMAS FOR COUNSELORS

Although not all differences in ethical orientation present an ethical problem for a school counselor, those that Ms. Hahn faces with the Chiantis and Dufeks are illustrations of two that do. In her previous experiences in working with parents and teachers, Ms. Hahn's conception of the problem and what would constitute a solution were shared by all those involved. The differences in perspective did not interfere in any important way as she worked with them toward a solution. What distinguishes these cases is that, from the counselor's perspective, the sources of Angela's and Janek's predicaments are the value orientations of their parents, whereas what bothers the parents about the school are things that Ms. Hahn sees as satisfactory and positive for the healthy development of children.

The ethical problem for Ms. Hahn is that she sees the possibility of harm coming to Angela as a direct result of the Chiantis' value orientation. She hesitates to say or do anything that would be seen as an attack on a client's religion or other fundamental convictions, but, at the same time, she has trouble ignoring the possibility of harm. Should she try to find some way to express her concerns to Ms. Chianti as they explore the options for Angela's education? Mr. Dufek, for his part, challenges Ms. Hahn's liberal, optimistic view of the public school. With whom can she consult about his concerns?

The Counselor's Ethical Obligations

Ethical dilemmas occur in situations where a person finds that acting in accordance with one ethical principle entails violating another. Ms. Hahn might be considering the following ethical obligations in this situation:

1. *A counselor's highest priority is to do whatever is reasonable to prevent harm and promote the welfare of the client.*
   Ms. Chianti may be my immediate client, but her chief concern, and the focus of our relationship, is Angela's welfare. Therefore, the first obligation in this case should be preventing harm to Angela.
2. *A counselor is ethically obligated to respect the religious beliefs of the client.*
   Whatever I decide to do to help Angela, I must be careful to avoid doing anything—except in an extreme situation—to suggest that the Chiantis' religious beliefs are false or unimportant.
3. *A counselor should recognize that the upbringing of children is primarily the responsibility of parents.*
   It would be much better for me to assist the Chiantis in making their own decisions about Angela's future, rather than telling them what I think they should do.
4. *A counselor is ethically obligated to be truthful.*
   In this situation, I am not required to tell Ms. Chianti my own views regarding Angela's problem or what I think should be done about it,

but this does not mean that it would be morally acceptable to deceive her.

5. *Counselors are ethically obligated to be attentive and empathetic listeners. They should try to see the situation from the client's point of view, and help clients make their own assessments of and decisions for dealing with their problems.*
   This suggests that my role in this case is to help Ms. Chianti determine *from her perspective* whether it would be better for Angela to remain in public school or move to parochial school. I should help her identify what *she sees* as the advantages and disadvantages of each option.
6. *It is ethically wrong for counselors to impose their own values on a client.*
   I think that Angela is doing just fine in this school, and changing schools now would harm her. Further, I believe that as individuals grow up, they should be encouraged to explore various religions and make independent judgments regarding their teachings. It is a woman's personal choice to decide whether she wants to pursue a professional career, to have a home and children, or to do both. I think it is wrong for parents to impose limits on a child's aspirations and right to foster independence and resourcefulness in children, encouraging a healthy skepticism about all matters including religion. This is how the situation appears from my perspective, but the Chiantis are seeing things from quite a different point of view. I do not think it would be right for me to try to make Ms. Chianti see the situation as I see it and to respond to it as I would. Still, rational dialogue may be possible not only about the important surface issues, but also about those that lie deeper.
7. *A counselor is sometimes justified in attempting to widen the moral outlook of a client.*
   Ms. Chianti's fundamental beliefs are not inviolable, and it is part of the educational dimension of counseling that they be probed. Of course, how and when to engage in such inquiry is a matter of sensitive judgment. Ms. Chianti might react quite negatively at first, but my questions might plant seeds that will blossom some time from now. In principle at least, there is no harm in Ms. Chianti hearing that there are alternative views to her own.

Ms. Hahn's ethical problem is to find a way to respond to Ms. Chianti that is compatible with all of these principles or, if this is not possible, to determine which of them takes precedence. In most of her cases, Ms. Hahn has been able to find effective actions to help her clients that have conformed with all the principles she saw as relevant to the case.

Where conflicts have arisen, she has had little difficulty in deciding which principles should be given highest priority. For example, when a client admitted that he had sexually abused a child, she told him that the child protection agency must be notified, and if he were unwilling to do it, she would. She was not abandoning her commitment to being an empathetic listener and helping the client to find his own way to deal with the situation, but removing the child from danger became her first concern.

What troubles Ms. Hahn about the Chianti case is her own view of the situation. She thinks that they are about to make a decision that is ill-advised and could result in harm to Angela. But she recognizes that the potential damage is not of an obvious kind that virtually any rational person would recognize, like child abuse or drug addiction. Here the potential harm is more elusive and diffuse. Of course, she is not alone in her judgment. It is rooted in basic values that are espoused and strongly supported by many thoughtful advocates. However, she recognizes that the harm Ms. Chianti sees in the public school program and the conception of the good life she is seeking for her daughter also stem from a value orientation that is supported by many other thoughtful persons.

Now Ms. Chianti is asking for her help in determining the best way to provide for Angela's long-term welfare, and she is not sure how to respond. Here are the ethical questions about the case that are troubling her:

- Am I certain that removing Angela from public school would be harmful to her and that the harm would be serious enough to make me ethically obligated to try to prevent it? If my view of Angela's situation is no more than a personal bias, I do not think I would be ethically justified in interfering with decisions her parents make regarding her upbringing.
- Now that I recognize that Ms. Chianti and I have conflicting value orientations and that they are relevant and quite important to the concerns that led her to seek counseling, are there actions that I am ethically obliged to take? Should I refer her to another counselor whose value orientation will be closer to hers? Should I reveal my convictions in this matter and let her decide if she wants to continue working with me?
- I am strongly committed to promoting the autonomy of my clients and to respecting their religious and other basic beliefs. Does this obligate me to try to keep my own value orientation entirely out of my discussions with Ms. Chianti? Should I try to avoid any com-

ments or questions that might be construed as a challenge to her value perspective? On the other hand, perhaps my commitment to autonomy means that I am obligated to help Ms. Chianti see all of the implications of her decisions regarding Angela's welfare as clearly as possible, and I should raise questions about my concerns.

- What does my commitment to promoting truth oblige me to do in this situation? Does it mean that I should reveal my views to Ms. Chianti or that I should try to exclude them altogether? Does it commit me to providing her with honest reactions as she considers various alternatives regarding Angela's future and their implications?

We have analyzed Angela's case in some detail. A similar treatment could be applied to Janek's case, though some of the particulars would differ. In the former, Ms. Hahn looks outward, as it were, to examine Ms. Chianti's religious views. In the latter, her focus shifts inward to the school. She must sift through the rhetoric surrounding public school education and sort out its real from its imaginary achievements, its intended from its unintended consequences. Finally, she needs a critical and realistic assessment of various plans for home schooling.

Preparation for Dealing with Ethical Problems

Let us consider, in a more general way, what school counselors can do to prepare themselves to deal with ethical problems related to value orientations. Counselors need to become as familiar as possible with their own value orientations. What is the ultimate source of value? How can one establish that something is good or evil? What is true about human nature? Are there some fundamental differences between the natures of human males and females? What are the characteristics of a good life? What sorts of moral obligations do people have to each other? What is the source of these commitments? Answering such questions is the process by which the foundation of a person's value orientation is constructed. However, because they are such basic questions, few individuals address them in a systematic manner. We have been at pains to argue that these issues ought not to be the exclusive province of philosophers and theologians; they are an integral part of any practical enterprise like counseling.

Self-analysis of values. Perhaps the best way for us to gain an understanding of our own value orientations is to reflect on our experiences and their effect on our beliefs about good and bad. Once we have identified some of our currently held values, we can consider the bases on which we hold them; that is, we can look for more fundamental values that underlie those closer to the surface. Ms. Hahn believes that parents should not impose limitations on the aspirations of their children. If she would ask herself why it is undesirable for parents to do this, she would begin to uncover some of her beliefs about the characteristics of a good life. From this kind of introspection, the patterns of our own value orientation will emerge.

It is important, for several reasons, for persons generally, and school counselors specifically, to identify and analyze their own fundamental values. For one thing, individuals are likely to discover inconsistencies that need to be addressed and resolved. A father who espouses the principle of equality of treatment might claim that it is very important for his son, but not his daughter, to complete a college education. A teacher might think that the students in her advanced placement class deserve much more time and attention than those in her regular groups. In exploring the bases of these beliefs, individuals may be able to reconcile the apparent contradictions, or may discover that they are unjustifiable and need to be revised. Another benefit of this kind of self-analysis is that it helps one become aware of personal biases. Ms. Hahn, for example, recognizes that her value orientation includes a bias against religious directives about what people should and should not do.

Perhaps the most important reason for an analysis of one's value orientation is to try to distinguish those beliefs about what is desirable and undesirable that are merely matters of personal or group preferences from those that rest on a sound moral foundation. For example, it might be fruitful for Ms. Hahn to investigate her reservations about the local parochial school. Perhaps she would discover that some of her concerns were unfounded or exaggerated.

Analysis of the school community. It seems equally important for school counselors to learn as much as possible about the value orientations prevalent in the school community. The more they can learn about the basic attitudes of the local families that are their prospective clients, the more likely it is that they can work effectively with them. What religious and ethnic groups are represented in the school? What do they see as the most important things for their children? Do they have different expectations for boys and girls? Do fathers or mothers tend to dominate family life? Are children allowed to participate in family decision making? Familiarity with the value perspectives represented in the community enables counselors to understand more fully the problems that clients bring to counseling sessions and to help them find ways of dealing with these issues that clients see as appropriate. Of course, in doing this, the counselor must be wary of stereotyping prospective clients.

If Ms. Hahn had known more about the prevalent attitudes of groups in her school community, she would still have been confronted with the problem she now faces, but at least Ms. Chianti's concerns would not have come as a surprise. Also, she could have given some thought to the problems she might encounter when working with parents whose views on child raising were different from her own.

Recognition of Ethical Problems

The most serious danger of lack of familiarity with one's own value orientations and alternatives is the failure to recognize ethical problems related to value orientations when they arise. Some school counselors have virtually unlimited confidence in their own ability to diagnose the problems of clients and to recommend proper remedial actions. They may simply assume that their perspective of the client's situation is the only accurate one and dismiss alternatives as the unfortunate results of personal or cultural prejudices. School counselors who have this attitude may be completely unaware of the kinds of problems we are discussing here, but that does not mean that they do not have them. This kind of ignorance can be very damaging.

Regardless of how much forethought a school counselor gives to value orientations, problems develop like the one Ms. Hahn is facing. They arise when, at some point in working with a client, the counselor recognizes that three conditions are present:

1. The counselor and the client see the situation from quite different perspectives. As discussed previously, this condition does not necessarily mean that the counselor has an ethical problem.
2. From the counselor's point of view, the client's perspective is a threat to someone's welfare. It appears that either the client or someone else is being harmed, or is likely to suffer injury because of the way the client sees the situation.
3. The counselor lacks confidence in the objectivity of his or her own assessment of the situation. It is essential for this condition to be present because it is very possible for counselors to be in a situation in which the first and second conditions exist, yet they have no ethical problem stemming from value orientations. For example, suppose a counselor is working with a student's parents who openly admit that their disciplinary measures include ridicule, beatings, and long periods

of solitary confinement. It is easy to imagine that the value orientations of counselor and client will conflict and that the counselor will assess the situation as dangerous for the child. Yet it is quite unlikely that ethical uncertainty related to value orientations will arise because research has established that child-rearing practices of this kind are harmful. The counselor can take some action to protect the child without extended analyses of the value orientations involved.

It is more difficult to provide guidelines for dealing with some problems than it is for others because the personal attitudes and convictions of an individual counselor are directly involved. For example, in a counseling session someone may reveal information that triggers repugnance in the counselor. For example, the client is a dedicated neo-Nazi or has sexually abused a child. Many counselors may be able to maintain productive rapport with the client under these circumstances. But others, after much introspection, may come to the conclusion that the client's revelation is so appalling that they cannot offer effective counseling services.

Responding to Ethical Problems

In spite of this difficulty, let us consider how counselors might reasonably respond when they realize that a value-orientation problem exists:

1. Counselors can do their best to understand the issue from the client's perspective. What does the client see as the crux of the problem? What are the value convictions of the client that underlie this conception? What does the client see as the best ways to deal with the dilemma? What are the values that lead the client to see these actions as desirable? As counselors accumulate answers to these questions, they can grasp something of the client's value orientation. Apparently, Ms. Hahn is very aware of what is troubling the Chiantis and Dufeks and the value orientations that underlie their perspectives.
2. Counselors can identify as clearly as possible just what it is about a client's value perspective that they find troubling. This task is less difficult for those counselors who have a good grasp of their own value orientation than for those who do not. Ms. Hahn understands quite well that she is troubled about the Chiantis' view of what is good for Angela and the religious basis for this view, and she does not share the Dufeks' critical assessment of school policy and practice.
3. Counselors can do their best to determine the basis for their con-

cerns and justifications. It is important for counselors to try to determine whether their concerns have an objective and substantial basis or are merely personal biases. Ms. Hahn might consider some questions such as

> What exactly is the harm I think will befall Angela if she moves to the parochial school? Clearly, parochial schools graduate many students who are independent thinkers and personally resourceful, qualities I think are so desirable; is there something about the particular school in which Angela would be enrolled that troubles me? If so, what goes on there that I think is undesirable, and what evidence do I have of this? I recognize that I am also troubled by the Chiantis' conception of the role of women, which they want to pass on to Angela. Do we merely have different biases regarding the role of women, or is one of our conceptions ethically sounder?

In the Dufek case, Ms. Hahn might ask what harm she thinks would befall Janek if he were receiving his education at home. She remembers vaguely that John Stuart Mill never spent a day in a public educational institution until he entered Cambridge. She knows that there are many other less famous cases. What kind of education could the Dufeks offer? What are the prospects for Janek's broad social, physical, and intellectual development?

4. Based on this analysis, the available options, and their probable results, counselors can make judgments about the best ways of handling situations. Such a judgment may be that the problem is not serious enough to require any remedial action. At the other end of the spectrum, the harm may be so apparent that immediate intervention is justified.

Selecting an appropriate response to an ethical problem related to value orientations requires counselors to do a self-assessment to determine their ability to work with a given client. An assessment of the client is also necessary for selecting an appropriate response. The client may be sophisticated or naive, open- or closed-minded, self-confident or insecure and assertive or retiring. Some clients may find it very helpful for the counselor to offer a viewpoint different from their own. They may be able to sift through the ideas offered by the counselor and incorporate some of them into their own perspective, while being able to reject others and give good reasons for doing so. Other clients may consider any suggestions by the counselor that are not compatible with their value orientation as personal attacks. Still others might want to avoid thinking about their problem entirely and solicit the counselor just to tell them what to do. Thus, whether or not to engage in a rational exchange of ideas may be a matter of strategic judgment, and is not ruled out in principle.

Let us consider some of the actions Ms. Hahn might decide to take in the case of Angela arising from her value-orientation problem:

1. She could suggest to Ms. Chianti that it might be better for her to discuss what would be in Angela's long-term interest with a priest or a counselor who has a value orientation similar to her own. Ms. Hahn could do this without revealing what she finds distressing in Ms. Chianti's viewpoint or how her own viewpoint differs. This course of action would be a way of showing respect for her client's value orientation. It would also be a way of avoiding anything that could be construed as an attack on the client's religion or convictions about proper child raising.

   However, in taking this action, Ms. Hahn would be relinquishing the opportunity to influence the Chiantis to take actions that she sincerely believes are in Angela's best interests. She might have decided her concern for Angela's welfare could be based on her own—perhaps unexamined—value orientation, rather than on moral reasoning and relevant evidence. She also might have decided that the gap between her own point of view and Ms. Chianti's is too great to be overcome, and that it would thus be pointless to bring it up.
2. She could continue to counsel Ms. Chianti but try to keep her own perspective entirely out of the discussions. That would mean exploring the options regarding Angela from Ms. Chianti's perspective. Ms. Hahn might raise some questions and make some suggestions that would be helpful to Ms. Chianti in clarifying her own values and choosing actions consistent with them, but she would raise no questions and make no suggestions that stemmed from her own value perspective. It would probably be difficult for Ms. Hahn to completely suppress her own views, but this course of action, like the first option, would be a way for her to show a kind of passive respect for her client's value orientation. Like the first option, it would also mean that Ms. Hahn would make no attempt to enlarge or modify Ms. Chianti's perspective on the situation, and that she would ignore her own concerns regarding Angela's welfare.
3. Ms. Hahn could raise the fact that Ms. Chianti has a perspective on Angela's situation that is quite different from her own and that she hesitates to help Ms. Chianti decide what to do because she recognizes that some of their basic values are incompatible. If Ms. Chianti

were receptive, she could point out some important differences in their viewpoints. She would then leave it to Ms. Chianti to decide whether she wants to select another counselor with more compatible views or continue working with her. If they agreed to continue working together, Ms. Hahn would not likely think it necessary to divulge all of her basic value convictions, but she could raise questions about the situation and about actions Ms. Chianti was considering.

This response would show regard for the autonomy of the client. Ms. Hahn would be helping Ms. Chianti see that there may be a problem in the counseling relationship and giving her the opportunity to terminate it. It would also indicate a respect for truth, for Ms. Hahn would be admitting that she might have some beliefs that could interfere with productive counseling and is revealing this possibility to her client so Ms. Chianti can make a more informed decision about continuing the relationship.

If Ms. Hahn takes this option, opportunities may arise for her to reveal her concerns and to bring some of her own ideas into the discussion. However, if she is too forceful, it could be interpreted as an attack on the religious and other basic value convictions of the client or an attempt by the counselor to impose her own perspective on the client's situation.

4. Regardless of what form the counseling relationship takes, Ms. Hahn might decide that she is ethically obligated to take some more direct action regarding Angela's long-term welfare. She would probably recognize that raising children and determining what sort of education is best for them is primarily the responsibility of parents, so her best opportunity to do something to help Angela would be to influence her parents. Let us assume that Ms. Hahn has a strong conviction that independence and resourcefulness are important qualities for both young men and women to develop and that women should have the same opportunities as men to select and pursue careers. Ms. Hahn might then share these views with Ms. Chianti and invite her to consider them in making decisions about Angela's future.

   Earlier, we learned that Ms. Hahn considered her highest ethical priority to be Angela's happiness and well-being. If she takes this option, she would be acting in accordance with this priority. She would probably recognize that, in doing so, she would be going beyond the normal role of school counselor and would be more an advocate for Angela than a facilitator for her client. This action could be interpreted as an imposition of the counselor's agenda and values. It could also be interpreted as an honest attempt to help the client understand the long-range implications of actions she is considering.

You will note that these options are not entirely exclusive of one another, and that Ms. Hahn might consider others. What is critical is that these and other alternatives be based on sound ethical premises.

SUMMARY

This chapter has described what value orientations are and how they develop, and has addressed the ethical problems related to conflicting value orientations. Counselors, clients, and even school communities have value orientations, and it is virtually inevitable that counselors will find themselves at some time or another in a value dilemma.

The cases of Angela and Janek are examples of the problem. Various options are available, and readers are invited to identify, explain, and justify what they would do in Ms. Hahn's position.

As a further exercise in ethical thinking, it might be interesting to modify the case somewhat to see if the changes make an alternate course of action more ethical. For example, suppose that the Chiantis' point of view was even more sexist than described. Suppose that they saw no reason for girls to continue their education beyond the minimum required by law. Suppose, further, that Angela is now 16, and her records indicate strong academic potential, yet her parents intend to withdraw her from school. Would this new information change the ethical obligations of the school counselor and suggest a different course of action as more ethically justifiable? In Janek's case, suppose that Ms. Hahn believes that, although Mr. Dufek's criticisms of the public school are valid, he would be incapable of implementing a credible alternative. Or, in all cases where she thought parents could do a better job than the school, would she be justified in actively promoting home schooling?

CHAPTER 3

The School Counselor and Ethical Dilemmas

Mr. Thompson, an elementary school counselor for several years, was recently transferred to Hilltop School. He is in his mid-40s and has raised two children without major problems. When his children were growing up, he and his partner showed them love and consideration and exerted only minimal pressure on them to excel in their school work. Neither parent saw any need to resort to corporal punishment or other drastic measures to encourage the academic, social, or moral development of their children.

Mr. Thompson quickly discovered that Hilltop School is quite unlike his last school, which had been in a predominantly white, upper-middle-class, suburban community where child-raising attitudes and practices were similar to his own. Hilltop, by contrast, is located in the central part of the city. It is a truly multicultural school; most children come from white or African-American backgrounds, but many are from Hispanic and Asian families.

It is clear to Mr. Thompson that virtually all the parents of his students genuinely love their children and want the best for them, but that they hold a wide range of views about the right way to raise them. Mr. Thompson recognizes that there are many cultural differences regarding child-rearing practices, and he thinks it is wrong for white, middle-class educators and counselors to try to impose their values on the multicultural community.

He has completed a session with Jason Park, a small, slight, third-grade student. Jason's teacher is concerned about his listlessness in class, his apparent anxiety, and his poor social adjustment. The school records show that his academic ability is high, but his achievement scores are well below average. Mr. Thompson has administered a series of tests which confirmed his own informal assessment. Jason rates low in self-esteem and high in anxiety. Mr. Thompson is also concerned about Jason's physical health. He is a frail child and seems to be chronically fatigued.

Mr. Thompson has tried several times to arrange a meeting with Jason's parents but has been unsuccessful. When he has called the home, Jason's mother has told him that Mr. Park is the one to talk to. When he finally reached Jason's father, Mr. Park made it plain that he wants as little interaction with the school as possible. In clear terms, he expressed his hostility toward the counselor, Jason's teacher, and especially the school program. He said he was so dissatisfied with the wishy-washy, watered-down curriculum and the lack of attention to discipline that he had decided to take control of Jason's education himself.

From discussions with Jason and his teacher, Mr. Thompson has learned that Mr. Park has purchased a large number of junior and senior high school textbooks and is making Jason work at least 3 hours every evening on a program he has devised. If Jason's attention and effort do not meet his father's standards, the study time is increased. If the expanded study time conflicts with dinner, then Jason misses dinner.

Mr. Thompson is not sure what he can do to help Jason. He considers calling the local child protection agency, but does not think he has sufficient grounds to initiate a child abuse investigation. (Jason has no physical signs of abuse, like cigarette burns or bruises.) If an investigation were conducted, it might do more harm than good—no doubt Mr. Park's hostility toward the school would be pushed to an even higher level, and life could become even tougher for Jason.

Mr. Thompson decides that the seriousness of Jason's situation and his own inability to determine what to do justifies a discussion of the problem with Ms. White, the school principal. Ms. White is quite familiar with the family. She has had several heated encounters with Mr. Park. Her view is that there is nothing to be done, and she makes it clear that she does not want Mr. Thompson to report the case because "it would only lead to more hostile confrontations with Mr. Park."

Mr. Thompson is not convinced that doing nothing at all is the right decision, but what can he do?

* * *

In Chapter 1, it was noted that a school counselor is compelled to make many value judgments, and the case of Maria was used to clarify what is involved. Chapter 2 demonstrated that value orientations are pervasive in making value decisions, although not all such orientations are subjected to careful, rational scrutiny. Here, Jason's situation will illustrate what makes some of the value problems faced by school counselors ethical problems.

To say that something or some action has value is to claim that it is good in some way. However, the concept "value" is a very broad one. We value things for many different reasons. A book may be valued for the pleasure or instruction it provides. A tool is usually valued for making some task easier. One's job may be valued for personal fulfillment, its social interactions, or as a means to make money. Values can be categorized in many different ways, such as the aesthetic, spiritual, and economic.

DISTINGUISHING ETHICAL VALUES

Ethical values are those values that pertain to human conduct. Actions are considered ethically good when they show appropriate regard for the interests of persons, animals, or the environment (though this book concerns only the first). Actions that lack this regard are considered unethical. Of course, there can be controversy in many situations regarding the particulars of what is and what is not appropriate regard for a person's interests. The source for such concern may be derived from custom, law, and social and employment commitments, but for it to be considered ethical, it must be drawn from an even broader context—our obligations to other persons as persons.

For example, it is customary to return books one has borrowed, and it is usually good business practice to keep promises made to customers. However, people properly assume that the act of borrowing a book or making a promise involves an obligation. If one has made a commitment to another, compelling ethical reasons are needed to override the commitment. Whether the commitment was made to a family member, a business associate, or a complete stranger does not substantially affect the obligation to act as one has promised. We keep promises because doing so is acting with proper regard for persons, and we are indignant toward those who unjustifiably break their promises to us because, quite apart from the inconvenience caused, we think such conduct shows a lack of regard.

A basic requirement of ethics is the recognition that we have obligations to others and ourselves as persons, and, thus, we cannot simply act selfishly or in ways that are self-demeaning. We are obliged to consider the welfare of others in planning our actions and assessing their consequences. We are obliged to recognize that others are striving to achieve their ends just as we are striving to achieve ours. It is insufficient to see others merely as means to our own ends. Equally, we are more than the means by which others gain their own ends. Either of these situations would constitute a kind of ethical slavery.

Freedom and Responsibility

Note that this fundamental requirement of ethics is based on an assumption about human conduct: that we have some degree of control over how we act. Kant's assumption about human freedom is that our actions are not entirely the result of physiological forces, drives, habits, or Pavlovian responses. This is the "presumption of human freedom." In many situations, we are capable of considering a number of possible alternatives, assessing their probable consequences, selecting the course of action that appears most desirable, and executing it. In these circumstances, we choose our actions and are said to be *responsible* for them.

We would have no ethical responsibility if we had absolutely no understanding of the connection between actions and their consequences. That is why we sometimes describe the behavior of infants as "good" or "bad," but never as "ethical" or "unethical." To act ethically or unethically, one must have some requisite understanding. To view someone from the moral point of view is to attribute to them a modicum of understanding and a presumption of freedom. On this basis we assign them attendant responsibilities.

In assessing someone's ethical responsibility, determining whether the person had sufficient understanding of alternatives and consequences and sufficient freedom to choose how to respond can be a difficult task. Factors that affect the ability to understand connections between actions and consequences include maturity, experience, education, and one's mental and emotional state. Many factors can limit one's ability to act freely, of which some are external (such as disabilities and poverty) and others internal (such as compulsions and addictions).

In some situations, people use lack of understanding of the connections between their behavior and its consequences as a reason why they should not be held responsible for some harmful result of their actions. When someone wants to hold a person accountable for the harm resulting from an action, this kind of defense may be offered: "Gee, I didn't realize things would turn out that way." This sort of disclaimer is sometimes reasonable. Human actions are complex and often have bizarre results that no one could have anticipated. Someone who does not accept a disclaimer is likely to say, "You *should* have known better than to have done that." This, too, can be a reasonable claim when the negative results of an action were quite predictable.

Similarly, people sometimes use lack of freedom as the reason they should not be held responsible for the harmful result of an action. When brought to account, a person might say, "I had no choice in the matter;

I had to do it." In some situations, this can be a reasonable claim. Perhaps the person was subject to some kind of irresistible force or coercion. Those who do not accept the explanation are likely to label it as mere rationalization for choosing an expedient course of action. Which of these claims is more justified could be very difficult to discover.

Perhaps the most important distinction between ethical values and other values is that the former are matters of principle. People act with various purposes in mind: achieving financial gain, comfort, popularity, or prestige are some. Acting on an *ethical* principle is different. In order to do what is required to fulfill our obligations to persons, we are obliged to respect standards based on ethical commitments, even as we pursue other purposes and seek other values. We would doubt a person's commitment to an ethical value, like keeping promises, if we noted that it faltered whenever it came into conflict with other values and desires, like expediency or popularity. One is obliged to act on ethical principles even when doing so results in some personal loss or discomfort. Of course, a commitment to an ethical value need not be limitless. When one ethical value, like truth telling, comes into conflict with another, such as preventing harm, we have an "ethical dilemma" and must try to establish which commitment takes precedence.

It is also important to remember that one's own well-being should be considered. Generally, people are not expected to be martyrs to retain the label of "ethical person." Being prudent in regard to personal interests is not unethical when nothing else is at stake; however, this is not a justification for abandoning moral commitments whenever they conflict with self-interest.

Along with observing the features that distinguish ethical values from other types, it is important to note the ways they are similar. All the characteristics of values discussed in Chapter 1 also apply to ethical values, and ethical judgments share the features of other value judgments. Let us review some of the more important aspects of ethical values while keeping these specific categories in mind.

Ethical values are not matters of mere preference or taste that can be selected like a necktie or a pair of earrings; nor can they be established solely on the basis of empirical information. Facts by themselves do not reveal what is ethically right or wrong. Ethical standards are necessary to establish the implications of the facts for human conduct. This does not mean that empirical information is unimportant in determining what is ethical. For example, the discovery that second-hand smoke can be very damaging has serious ethical implications for smokers because it has harmful consequences for others. When confronted with an ethical problem, one may not be sure about the best course of action, but the question cannot be reasonably decided in some arbitrary way, like rolling dice. Making an ethical judgment involves considering the alternatives available for action, the likely consequences of each, and the ethical implications.

In the Case of Jason

Mr. Thompson's case provides an example. His situation is similar to that of Ms. Larkin's in Chapter 1. Several lives will be seriously affected by what he decides, even if he decides to do nothing. It is not at all clear what his choice should be.

If he were willing to act on the basis of narrow self-interest or expediency, the matter could be settled quickly and easily: he should follow the advice of his principal, Ms. White, and bend to the demands of Mr. Park. This "solution" might enable him to avoid heated confrontations and personal stress.

Another easy option would be to refer the problem to someone else in the bureaucracy. He could reason that, as Ms. White is his superior, she should handle it any way she wants. He might also be able to distance himself from the problem by placing it on the desk of the director of counseling services at the school board office, or by reporting the case to a child protection agency and letting officials there determine what to do.

It would not be surprising if Mr. Thompson's first thoughts were about how to dump the problem in the quickest and least personally stressful way. Many people in such situations are inclined toward expediency and self-interest. However, let us assume that Mr. Thompson has a well-developed sense of ethical responsibility. He recognizes that his actions are likely to affect the well-being of several other persons, so ethically he cannot limit his thinking to what is expedient or in his own interest. He feels obliged to consider what responsibilities he has to others, to weigh his options carefully, and to assess how others will be affected by various actions.

Resolving what to do might involve Mr. Thompson in the following kinds of deliberation:

- Before I decide, I want to have all possible relevant information. I had better see if I can learn more about Jason's physical condition. Maybe the school nurse can help me. Perhaps I should also seek more information about Jason's family and their cultural background. Maybe stern child-raising practices are common in that group. I had better talk further with Jason's teachers, who may have more specific information about his problems. I wonder to what extent Mr. Park's complaints about the poor quality of the school program are true. Have accusations been made by other parents?

- Clearly, my first concern should be Jason's welfare. He is my client, and he is young and vulnerable. His teachers and Ms. White have the educational needs of many children to consider, and they lack the training and experience that I have in assessing the psychological and emotional well-being of children. No doubt Mr. Park has the best intentions for Jason, but his understanding of the likely effects of his actions seems quite limited. If I have good reasons to believe that conditions exist that jeopardize Jason's chances of growing up in a healthy manner and his chances of gaining the most out of his school experiences, surely I should try to do something about it.
- However, I should remember that this is a multicultural community, and child-rearing practices among the various groups are likely to be quite different. I should also keep in mind that, in this society, raising a child is considered to be primarily the responsibility of parents. The views of Jason's parents should be respected. I have no right to intervene just because their ideas about good family practices differ from my own middle-class views. Before I take any action that is likely to bring unwanted public attention to the family or weaken the family bonds, I had better be sure that the action is well justified.
- Jason is 10 years old; clearly, he is not mature enough to assume total responsibility for assessing the situation and determining what might be done. But he is entitled to contribute to important decisions about his own life. Maybe I should ask him for a more complete description of the situation from his perspective. What does he think are the reasons for a decline in his school work? How does he feel about the home education program that his father is imposing? What does he feel could be done to make life easier for him?

These are only some of the thoughts that are likely to go through Mr. Thompson's mind as he considers what he should do. However, they are enough to connect the previous discussion about ethical values with Mr. Thompson's situation.

We can begin by noting that Jason's case meets the basic requirements for engaging in ethical action. Mr. Thompson is a rational adult, capable of deliberating about a situation, deciding what to do, and being responsible for his decision. We should also note that he has genuine choices in this situation. Ms. White and Mr. Park are exerting pressure on him to make certain decisions, but it would be stretching the truth to say that they are compelling him. Mr. Thompson is ethically responsible for whatever he decides to do to help Jason. This does not mean that, if some harm results from his actions, we can reasonably conclude that his actions were unethical. The results of actions are often complex. How one's actions will affect others and how others will respond to them is never entirely predictable. We cannot expect omniscience from Mr. Thompson, only good intentions and reasonable judgments based on the information available at the time.

Mr. Thompson recognizes that he has obligations to other persons. His primary concern right now is Jason, but he is also considering whether he has ethical obligations to Jason's parents and to Ms. White. His deliberations also indicate his recognition that his ethical obligations take precedence over expediency or personal desires. He is not satisfied simply to seek the easiest and least personally stressful path to remove himself from the problem.

It is clear that Mr. Thompson's problem is an ethical one. He believes that as a school counselor, he must recognize and be guided by important ethical obligations such as the following:

- Do everything within the limits of the position to prevent harm from coming to students and to enable students to acquire the best education possible.
- Abide by the law, school board policies, and the authorized directives of superiors in the school system.
- Recognize that students are persons and, as such, should have an important role in determining how to deal with their problems and establishing directions in their lives.
- Recognize that parents have the primary responsibility for raising their children and that their wishes should always be considered.

In many previous situations, tenets like these have enabled Mr. Thompson to determine that a course of action was ethically necessary or ethically unacceptable. But on this occasion, the appropriate application of his principles is unclear. It seems that acting in accordance with some of them may entail violating others. Mr. Thompson is facing an ethical dilemma, in which the equal application of his ethical commitments conflicts, and there is no course of action available that will not result in harm to someone.

THEORIES OF ETHICS

Mr. Thompson is trying to decide which of a number of possible courses of action is the most ethically justified. How can a person assess the ethical rightness or wrongness of an action? What makes one action ethically better or worse than another? Although many kinds of answers have been offered to these questions, this discussion will be limited to two of the most useful: consequentialist and deontological theories. Consequentialist theories suggest that we can determine the ethical correctness of an action by an analysis of its consequences; deontological theories contend that we can determine the value of human actions from universal principles of ethical conduct. Each theory has merit, but each has problems of application as well.

Consequentialist Theories

A common tenet of consequentialist theories of ethics is the belief that the value of an action should ultimately be determined by assessing its effect on the world. Actions are ethically desirable if they increase what is good or decrease what is bad. Actions that have the opposite results are ethically undesirable. Consequentialists differ about the kinds and the hierarchy of values in the world and, thus, differ about the appropriate foundation on which to appraise the ethics of actions. Hedonists, for example, believe that assessment should be made on the basis of pleasure and pain. When considering alternatives for action, the one that will result in the greatest balance of pleasure over pain is the ethically most desirable choice. Utilitarians hold that the general good of all humankind is the criterion one should use in evaluating the ethics of an action.

"Act utilitarians" maintain that the consequences of individual acts must be assessed to determine their ethical merit. "Rule utilitarians," on the other hand, hold that we need not make an individual ethical assessment of each act. Over time, they observe, precedents have evolved that establish what actions, in general, bring the most desirable results in a variety of situations, and ethical choices can be determined by reference to these rules.

This is not the appropriate place for a thorough examination of these theories. However, it would be helpful to see how a consequentialist approach might be used in situations like that of Mr. Thompson. Consequentialist ethics has a common sense appeal. Virtually every thoughtful person with a sticky problem—ethical or otherwise—tends to consider what the likely results of certain actions will be. A choice is then made on the basis of the relative value apparent in the results. Surely, Mr. Thompson will consider what the likely outcomes will be if he does nothing, calls the child protection agency, or takes some other course of action, and he will consider whether the results of the various alternatives will be helpful or harmful to Jason and his family.

However, there are some problems in deciding which action is best on the basis of consequences. It is often very difficult to predict who will be affected and in what way. Also, actions have both short- and long-range consequences. Is it better to do something that will be immediately beneficial to someone if the long-range results look bleak? Is it acceptable to cause some immediate suffering if the eventual prospects look promising? Suppose an action will benefit many people but cause suffering to a few—or cause great benefit to a few while only mildly damaging many? How does one decide which set of results are preferable?

Another problem with consequentialist ethics is the lack of clear criteria to use when trying to determine the value of the outcomes of various actions. In considering a new job in another city, for example, one would probably begin by assessing factors that are personally important, such as the increase in salary, the potential of the new job for personal satisfaction, and the attractiveness of the new environment. However, ethical persons would also consider the effects of a move on their families. It is quite possible for the results of this assessment to be mixed: Some might see the move as an exciting adventure; others might be very distressed to give up close friends and cherished activities. The increased income could bring a higher standard of living for the family, but the move might also mean that one's spouse has to give up a personally rewarding job or that one's adolescent daughter must dissolve bonds of friendship with schoolmates. Working out some kind of hierarchy of advantages and disadvantages on which to make a decision could be very difficult.

Mr. Thompson cannot be sure what consequences would follow the various actions he is considering. For example, if he calls the child protection agency, he is quite sure they will investigate Jason's situation at home, but he does not know what the results of the investigation would be. Furthermore, it is likely that the results could be a mixture of gains and losses. Mr. Park might be persuaded to ease up on Jason's home study program, but his hostility for the school program, Jason's teacher, and especially for Mr. Thompson might increase. Perhaps any chance of developing a fruitful relationship with him would be lost. The long-range consequences of this action would be even harder to assess.

Another problem emerges when we remember that Mr. Thompson has already identified several value standards that he believes are reasonable guides for deciding how to act. It would be fortunate but unlikely if he could find a course of action that would satisfy them all. It is more probable that he will have to decide which standards take priority over others. An analysis of the consequences of acting in accordance with each standard would be useful, but only if he has identified some higher standards or principles by which they can be assessed.

Deontological Theories

Deontologists believe that the way to determine the ethical rightness or wrongness of acts is on the basis of principles and rules, rather than an assessment of consequences. There are a variety of deontological theories, but it will be sufficient here to review some of Kant's ideas, one of deontology's most influential advocates. One of his basic assumptions was that all humans have intrinsic worth—that no person should be thought of (or used) merely as a means to someone else's ends. He believed that, through reasoning alone, principles and rules regarding how humans should treat each other can be established. In order for an ethical principle to be valid, it must be logically consistent and universalizable; that is, it must be evident that an action is right or wrong for all persons in similar circumstances. Kant used "promise keeping" as an example. If a promise were to be made with no intention of keeping it, or with the intention of keeping it only as long as it is expedient to do so, the whole point of promise keeping would be lost. It would be the equivalent of saying "I promise that I will do that, but I may break my promise at any time, so do not count on me doing what I said I would do." Clearly, this conception of promise keeping could not be universalized. People give and accept promises to provide assurance that some action will be performed. Take away that assurance and promise keeping has lost its meaning and purpose.

This provides some useful criteria for determining whether a way of acting is ethically justified and avoids the difficulties associated with the assessment of consequences. Actions are not ethically acceptable unless they conform to logically consistent and universalizable principles of good conduct.

It does not seem difficult to establish examples of some principles that meet these criteria:

> One should keep promises.
> One should tell the truth.
> One should not do harm to others.

Principles like these seem to present no logical inconsistencies and could be universalized without difficulty. Indeed, it would be a wonderful world if everyone lived by such principles.

However, problems arise when one tries to use them to deal with a complex situation like the one Mr. Thompson faces. What are the principles that apply to this specific situation? What does one do if two or more principles that seem clearly justifiable when considered separately happen to come into conflict when applied to the situation? For example, it is easy to concoct a scenario in which keeping a promise or telling the truth would result in serious harm to someone. I might promise to loan you my hunting rifle, only to discover later that you intend to do away with yourself or your spouse. One's inclination is to try to resolve such dilemmas by considering the consequences of keeping or not keeping a promise in a specific set of circumstances. However, deontologists rule this out.

Mr. Thompson has already identified some principles that he believes establish right conduct for school counselors. These principles seem to have more specific application than those identified as universal by the deontologists. Some logical connections could be made between principles at the two levels, but these connections are not obvious.

The idea that the ethical justification of actions should be determined, in the first instance, on the basis of logically consistent and universalizable precepts, rather than an assessment of consequences, is an appealing one. However, deontological theories tend not to provide satisfactory ways to resolve conflicts among principles or to show the logical connections between general principles and the lower level standards like the ones Mr. Thompson developed to guide him in his response to the Park family.

It should not be too surprising that neither the consequentialists nor the deontologists provide a theory that enables us to resolve ethical dilemmas easily. Such problems are often too complex to be solved in the way that one might solve a mathematical equation. Theories do no more than provide a lens through which to see ethical problems more clearly, and a framework to help us evaluate alternative responses to them. Both kinds of theories can be put to good use in addressing ethical problems. It seems patently sensible for counselors in such a situation to identify a number of plausible responses and consider what consequences are likely to follow. Further, counselors might also consider how these consequences will benefit or harm those affected by the responses suggested by consequentialist theories (e.g., pleasure–pain, human happiness, or well-established societal rules). However, the identification and justification of ethical principles relevant to the situation is crucially important for dealing with the problem. They establish the ethical significance of the various responses the counselor is considering and determine which consequences are ethically justified.

Ethical principles are also at the core of one's personhood. Often, an evaluation of the consequences of one's actions would benefit many, including oneself. A person may reject an action "on principle" because the price of securing an advantage would be to lie or to treat another unfairly. The extent to which an individual adheres to ethical principles defines his or her integrity.

SUMMARY

The case of Mr. Thompson and the Park family illustrates what it is like to have an ethical dilemma and provides the basis for briefly reviewing two theories that are helpful in addressing such problems. Consequentialist theorists maintain that the ethical justification of actions can be established by assessing their results, whereas deontologists claim that the ethical justification of actions can be established by reference to logically consistent and universalizable principles. Ethical values pertain to human conduct in which we have obligations to others, and the existence of these obligations is based on the assumption that we have some understanding of the connections between acts and their consequences as well as some degree of control over how we act. Such commitments are matters of principle and take precedence over personal desires and expediency. Ethical dilemmas occur in situations where ethical principles cannot be applied without conflict. Although ethical theories are useful for addressing ethical problems and evaluating possible responses, they cannot provide us with formulae for solving any specific ethical problem.

CHAPTER 4

Ethical Reasoning

The cases introduced in Chapters 1 and 3 provide us with a general idea of how ethical reasoning begins. When working with clients, both Ms. Larkin and Mr. Thompson recognized that they needed to make some decisions that would have significant effects on the lives of their clients and, perhaps, others as well. Both recognized that routine responses would not resolve the situation satisfactorily.

When difficult ethical problems arise, we are tempted to seek quick and easy resolutions. Alternatives to taking ethical responsibility spring quickly to mind: Ms. Larkin was inclined to contact Maria's family immediately, and Mr. Thompson recognized that he could avoid many hassles by refraining from action altogether. But the moral life requires us to resist these inclinations. No step-by-step procedures or magical formulae lead unerringly to a "right answer." Determining the most justified response to a complex situation requires careful and sustained thinking. We need to identify all viable responses and give careful consideration to the ethical implications of each. Some courses of action may be eliminated because they are impossible or prohibitively impractical. For example, Ms. Larkin may have momentarily considered giving all of her time and attention to helping Maria, but she soon realized that other commitments could not be ignored. Other ways of proceeding may be ruled out because they violate important moral principles. For example, Mr. Thompson quickly decided not to comply with his principal's request to ignore the plight of Jason.

AVOIDANCE

Many people are adept at avoiding serious thought in dealing with ethical problems. The following are three of the most common maneuvers and why they are unsatisfactory:

1. *Thinking about ethics is just a "head trip." My gut feelings tell me what I should and should not do.*

Some people believe that their consciences or viscera provide them with a moral compass. But unexamined feelings or impulses are not always reliable in identifying and addressing an ethical problem. This is not to denigrate the importance of intuitions in such situations. Recognition of a problem usually begins with a feeling of disequilibrium, a nascent or half-formed notion that something is just not right. An inclination to respond in a routine way may be blocked by a feeling of uneasiness. Feelings can serve as warning signals, but they do not tell us what the problem is or what response is ethically justified. For that, reflection is the only avenue. Those who claim that their feelings provide infallible ethical guidance would have a hard time persuading the rest of us to accept a decision merely because it feels right to them. Justification requires thinking.

2. *I don't have any ethical problems. I just do what it says I'm supposed to do in the job description.*

Job descriptions provide useful guidelines to follow, especially when one is new in a position; they indicate just what an employer expects of employees. However, they are unlikely to include any justification for these directives, and even if they do, it is likely to be in terms of what is practical rather than what is ethically justified. One is prudent to try to stay within such guidelines, but one cannot count on them for ethical leadership. In this century, we have many examples of people inflicting great harm on others while "just doing their jobs."

3. *If I have doubts about how to handle a situation, I just ask my supervisor.*

Another strategy involves transferring the responsibility for ethical decisions to someone else. The counselors' bureaucratic backsides might be covered, but shirking their moral duty to their clients would be exposed. In addition, the supervisor's advice, even when it is based on ethical reasoning, may be of inferior quality. For counselors to adjudicate advice, they have received requires that they do their own ethical thinking. Of course, one is wise to seek advice in a difficult situation, but this is quite different from slavishly following the dictates of others.

Thus, reasoning is indispensable in analyzing problems to determine the most morally justified response. We cannot count on intuitions, the views of others, customs, school policies, or state laws to tell us what we ought to do, although what we receive from these sources may be helpful.

ETHICAL PRINCIPLES

In Chapter 3, we established two assumptions about ethical reasoning: (a) acting ethically means acting in accordance with well-justified ethical principles, and (b) an analysis of the alternatives for action and their likely consequences are usually essential parts of the analysis of an ethical problem. Contributions from both the consequentialists and the deontologists are necessary but insufficient for settling an ethical problem.

In Chapter 3, Mr. Thompson recognized that acting ethically meant acting on the basis of relevant principles and so attempted to determine which ones should guide his actions. He had problems because he recognized that some of his convictions seemed to be in conflict. For example, he thought he was obliged both to protect Jason from harm and to respect the child-raising decisions of Jason's parents.

While alluding to ethical principles and their significance, we have until now offered very few details. Though moral agency (and, so, moral education) consists of more than using such principles to think about the world, they are central to moral experience. Such principles make ethical reasoning possible and provide it with a degree of objectivity.

Some might counter that these claims are too strong—all ethical values are relative to individuals or to cultures and, thus, ideas about ethical reasoning and objectivity are far-fetched. This criticism had its origins with the Greek sophists and includes in its philosophically respectable lineage the British empiricists (notably David Hume), the emotivists (notably Bertrand Russell and A. J. Ayer), and, currently, a raft of postmodernists. Forms of relativism are also present in some psychological theories (and in their humanistic counseling counterparts) and surface in highly individualistic injunctions such as "Do your own thing" and "If it feels right, it is right."

Counselors are more aware than most of the extraordinary diversity of values possessed by students in our multicultural schools; in an era of political correctness, counselors might easily succumb to pressure and view all values from whatever cultural source as on a par (no matter how homophobic, racist, or sexist). Counselors are especially vulnerable if they possess no philosophical understanding of ethical theory with which to combat social and cultural fashions.

On the other hand, others might express disappointment that these claims do not go far enough. Like Plato, they believe, or wish to believe, that moral thinking is akin to mathematical thinking in that they both provide definitive answers. A more reasonable approach is that moral reasoning is possible, but its conclusions are often uncertain.

Although this is not the place for a full-fledged defense of this middle ground, the sketch that follows may at least appear plausible to those who wrestle with the difficult challenges in counseling. The schema of ethical principles we outline should be useful in understanding moral experience in general and shed light on the dilemmas that counselors face in particular. Chapter 5 provides further clarification of each of the principles and discusses their application to ethical problems in counseling.

Respect for Persons: The Fundamental Principle

Respect for persons is an absolute, though formal, first principle of morality. To see others with respect is to see them from the moral point of view. Respect for persons transforms individuals from being objects—merely consumers, statistics, workers, casualties, impersonal sources of sexual gratification, and so on—into subjects at all times worthy of one's intrinsic positive concern. In a Kantian formulation, we are commanded not to treat persons simply as a means to our own ends but also as ends in themselves. The principle is absolute; no exceptions are permitted; it is to be applied universally; and it is not a matter of degree. From the moral point of view, then, we are all equally persons.

This definition should not be confused with other notions of persons. When we ask what sort of a person someone is, we are seeking a list of personal characteristics, only some of which might fall inside the moral domain. In another area, humanist psychologists assure us that we could each become more of a "real" person. At the apex of their developmental theories, they postulate a self that could be more realized or actualized than it is at present. Finally, you can report your respect for someone who is courageous, altruistic, or long-suffering, or who is an inspired painter, skilled mechanic, or powerful marathoner. In these instances, your admiration is evoked by an eminent degree of excellence or talent. In these cases, a value appraisal of some kind is made, and we may discover that, with respect to what is being judged, we are not all equal. People receive your accolades because, you say, they have earned them; by contrast, in the moral domain, personhood is simply bestowed.

Who, then, are "persons"? They are described minimally as those members of a species who are (under normal circumstances) capable, or potentially capable to some degree, of making decisions and life plans in a self-consciously, rational manner. (Although this formulation is abstract, it must be carefully rendered because it demarcates those whom it will cover. In this version, babies, the mentally retarded, and the senile would certainly be included.) The principle is formal in that it does not require any details about anyone's intelligence, appearance, ethnic background, wealth, gender, status, accomplishments, or even achieved moral attributes. Thus, from the moral point of view, being a person is not contingent upon a description of such things. It is not a discernible characteristic in the world to be observed about people, but rather a concept to be imposed on the world as a way of seeing them. We do not discover that people are persons—we make them so.

This may not seem like a very promising beginning, for the principle may appear too removed from practice to be useful, or so self-evident and uncontroversial as to be uninteresting. True, it does not provide direction in concrete situations, but that is because it is *part* of a theory, and not the whole of it. In any case, accusing the principle of being removed from practice is a little like criticizing an anchor for not being a ship's engine. An anchor prevents you from being dashed on the rocks; it also allows you to take your bearings without drifting. Respect for persons is similarly indispensable in the moral life.

The power of the principle can best be appreciated in areas where it is currently contested. Pro-life and pro-choice advocates know well that at the basis of their explosive dispute over abortion lies the question of the status of the fetus: Is it ever, or always, a person? In another domain, animal rights theorists and activists, over the past 20 years, have made us rethink our views about animals, especially gorillas, chimpanzees, whales, and dolphins: Should they be accorded the moral status of personhood? Those who struggle on either side of these two volatile issues know what is at stake. Those who are included within the concept of personhood will be accorded a range of valuable rights; the issue is anything but insignificant.

To many, the principle may now appear self-evident, though their view is hardly shared worldwide. In any case, we should guard against moral arrogance by remembering that our society's commitment to this principle is relatively recent. In the United States, slavery was abolished only a century and a half ago, and full civil rights were not extended to African Americans until this generation. Women were defined as persons in Canadian law only in 1929, and feminists have struggled ever since for the full implementation of this principle in the daily lives of women.

Note that in the examples developed thus far, Ms. Larkin, Ms. Hahn, and Mr. Thompson were clearly concerned about their clients as persons—that is, as centers of value in their own right. But the client is not the only one who might be affected by their decisions; parents and administrators, for example, are not just flies in the ointment, but also individuals with morally legitimate interests. Respect for persons obligates counselors to extend this concern, but it does not provide much assistance in establishing specific ethical obligations. Lower-level principles and rules are needed.

Second-Order Principles

The second-order principles that give direction to our general orientation toward human beings include: considering the interests of others, maximizing freedom, respecting the truth, and treating persons equally. They are objective, though not absolute. For this reason, they are called *prima facie* principles: They apply when "all things are equal"—that is, when no other principle is thought to override them. Thus, second-order principles can clash with one another when a concrete case is under consideration. For example, parents, teachers, and school counselors often have considerable difficulty applying to relationships with adolescents the principles of considering interests and maximizing freedom. They want to provide them with as much freedom as possible, while at the same time protecting them from harm.

When acting on a second-order principle, one is always manifesting respect for persons; thus, these two levels never conflict. But, as shown, actions justified by two different second-order principles may be incompatible. The scheme illuminates the situation with which we are all too familiar—the ethical dilemma. As the case studies demonstrate, counselors are familiar with this phenomenon.

Each of these principles is connected to respect for persons. Although they provide the general grounds for generating obligations, they are guides to thinking *about* action, rather than direct guides *to* action. Because the moral life is ultimately one of action, we need rules that encourage, permit, or prohibit classes of actions. In Western culture, the Ten Commandments is an example of one such set; counseling codes of ethics would be another. Deontologists also provide lists of such moral rules, such as, one ought to keep promises, tell the truth, and not harm others (see Chapter 3). These rules are rational when they are justified by higher order principles. In our three examples, we are not provided with any rational justification but asked to rely on the word of Moses (or the Word of God if one accepts the theology); on the deliberations of a professional, blue-ribbon committee; or—heaven forbid—on the intuitions of a philosopher (G. E. Moore in *Principia Ethica*, for example).

One characteristic of moral rules is that their validity often depends on contingent circumstances. They are general guides to behavior that can be overturned if acting under the rule would result in intolerable consequences. Therefore, one might

1. lie to prevent a rape;
2. permit voluntary euthanasia to end excruciating suffering;
3. restrict the freedom of a criminal to protect society;

and so on.

"Intolerable" in this context means that even though the action violates a second-order principle, the consequences are more serious if one *obeys* the original moral rules—

1. do not lie;
2. preserve life; and
3. maximize freedom of movement—

than if one does *not*, for then:

1. someone is raped;
2. another lives in inconceivable pain indefinitely; and
3. more people are the victims of crime.

What matters procedurally is that the moral rules, or codes of conduct, should not be separated from the higher order principles that are their justificatory lifeline.

Codes of conduct for counselors function like moral rules: They are intended to govern a counselor's actions. As a rule, they are severed from their sources of justification. As a result, their rational consideration—or reconsideration—is rendered impossible. Indeed, it is even difficult to interpret them because they are so removed from any context that could give them meaning. They amount to little more than platitudes for practice. This issue will be raised in greater detail in Chapters 7 and 9.

Consideration of interests. The logical connection between consideration of interests and respect for persons is quite easy to draw. Persons were defined as those who have the capacity to make decisions and life plans in a reasonably rational manner. The interests principle fills out an aspect of the formal principle by highlighting the general needs and desires of humans (a degree of security, health, and happiness, for example) which, when satisfied, make it possible to pursue more particular and idiosyncratic concerns. Given the requirement of being positively disposed toward persons and the content of their decisions and life plans, there is a general obligation to help others pursue both their general and more specific interests.

The general obligation created by the second-order principle does not shed any light on the degree of support one must provide to others. It is silent in regard to which persons have the greatest call on our time and energy (family, clients, or strangers on the street), and what channels we should use (personal or political, for example). These are decisions that have to be made at lower levels of moral reasoning that would take into account a number of contingent factors. The consideration of interests principle simply establishes the framework.

Another difficulty arises in applying this principle because it is not always clear what a person's legitimate interests are. Note the ambiguity of the concept of "interest": one can ask about someone's interests, and one can assess what is in that person's interest. The results of the two inquiries may be quite different. For example, we may inquire as to a 7-year-old's interests, and the enthusiastic response may be about a love of rollerblades, Big Macs, and Ninja Turtles. However, if we assess what is in the child's interest, we would probably identify items like a loving, secure home life; a nutritious diet; and a good education. It is an open question whether what one is interested in is in one's interests. What someone is interested in is a matter of biography; what is in one's interest is a normative matter. Of course, it is a happy coincidence when what one is interested in is in that person's interest. An academic counselor is happy when, having made the value judgment that second-language acquisition, mathematics, and science are in a student's interest, she or he finds that the client is enthusiastically choosing to take Japanese, calculus, and advanced physics. Because deciding what is in someone's interest has this normative component, there are value differences over what is worth pursuing and achieving.

Ms. Larkin, from Chapter 1, gave serious consideration to what Maria, her pregnant client, wanted her to do, but she also gave careful thought to whether it was in Maria's interest to inform her parents, even though this was contrary to Maria's wishes. Similarly, Mr. Thompson (Chapter 3) considered whether Mr. Park's educational plan for his son was in Jason's best interest, but he also decided to ask Jason about his view of his own interests. Both counselors showed genuine concern for the interests of their clients, but it was not an easy task to determine what those interests were in the situations their clients were facing.

Another difficulty connected with the application of this principle is that, quite often, several persons have a legitimate interest at stake. Note that this is true in both of the cases discussed above. The school counselors recognized that the parents of their clients had some justifiable concerns, even if those concerns were in conflict with those of their clients. It can happen that providing for the valid claims of one person may entail setting aside those of others, and it can be difficult determining whose interests should be given priority and providing ethical justification for this decision.

Maximizing freedom. The freedom principle is required because it provides people with the necessary "space" to exercise the essence of their moral being—that is, the capacity to make decisions and life plans. It would be logically inconsistent under normal conditions to claim respect for persons and then deny them the opportunity to act on their personhood. At this general level, the freedom principle provides the baseline for arguments against killing (which eliminates the possibility of all future action of any kind) and indoctrination (which restricts the capacity of a person to consider issues rationally) and supports positions that promote life, such as those, for example, in the Hippocratic Oath.

In the last section, it was suggested that showing respect for someone involves recognizing that that person has interests—needs, problems, goals, and life plans. A minimal interpretation of the freedom principle entails that one should simply refrain from interfering with an individual's choices on these matters. However, a more robust interpretation would include this noninterference requirement and add an obligation to do what one reasonably can to enable the person to make good and effective choices in life. This more demanding obligation is central to the educational enterprise as a whole, where it is justified to constrain a child's freedom now (through compulsory school attendance laws) in order to expand the maturing individual's freedom later.

It is also appropriate to apply the principle to the counselor-to-client relationship. For example, when working with rational adults, the counselor might show greater restraint in interfering with their deliberations and decisions about what they should do. However, if the counselor is working with a distraught adolescent, as in Chapter 1, the client may lack the emotional stability to be able to make a responsible decision. Perhaps the appropriate application of the principle would be to help the client see more clearly what options are available and what consequences would likely follow various actions, and even to offer concrete advice. The justification for this intervention could draw on both the freedom and consideration of interests principles.

Respect for truth. The presence and promotion of truth are necessary for making rational judgments. Thus, to lie is to disrespect persons, for it undermines their capacity to make wise and prudent decisions. Imagine trying to make life plans in a "mindscape" in which *nothing* that is heard, read, or seen could be relied on to be true. Would it be possible to make plans of any kind? The more radical formulation of this argument holds that were the conditions imagined here in effect, true propositions could not be learned and, thus, nothing could be known about the world. That is to say, understanding itself would be undermined. Rationality presupposes a commitment to truth within a society.

Therefore, respect for persons obligates us to refrain from intentionally deceiving others, to do our best to see situations clearly, and when appropriate, to report what we see accurately, and to respect the rules of evidence and logic when giving and weighing reasons. In a special relationship like that of counselor and client, the truth principle is especially central. Counselors should do everything they reasonably can to see the client's situation and problems clearly and to ensure that their clients also have a clear perspective. Note that in all of the school counseling cases previously discussed, the counselor demonstrated a concern for truth. Mr. Thompson wanted a medical opinion about Jason's physical condition to help him to decide the appropriate response to Jason's problems. Ms. Larkin decided to explore with Maria the basis for her belief that her father's reaction to her pregnancy would not be compassionate. Ms. Larkin's intent was to help Maria determine whether she had made an accurate assessment of her father's attitude. But the truth principle when applied to counseling requires more than ensuring that one knows certain facts accurately. Counselors have to wrestle also with the question of the perspective or framework within which the facts are arranged. It is the context that gives facts their significance or meaning—a point that feminist counselors make repeatedly and tellingly.

Treating persons equally (or impartially). Equality of treatment, a principle that protects persons against arbitrary and unexpected manipulation, is a requirement for making rational decisions and life plans. Again, imagine a world in which there was no impartiality. How could you plan for anything? What would be your chances of being successful? Given the minimal description of persons in the respect-for-persons principle, there could be no justification for treating anyone preferentially. When other contingent factors are included in making a concrete judgment, the equality principle amounts to a presumption that all persons should be given the same consideration unless there are relevant differences to justify differential treatment. The difficulty in applying the principle, of course, is in determining what kinds of differences justify giving someone special treatment.

We had a simple example of this problem in Chapter 1. As her scheduled time with Maria comes to an end, Ms. Larkin tries to decide if she should cancel her later appointments in order to continue her work with Maria. More specifically, she has to make an ethical decision: Does the seriousness of Maria's problem and her present emotional distress justify giving her more attention than those with later appointments? Mr. Thompson (Chapter 3) believes that the major responsibility for decisions about raising children belongs to parents and that counselors should not interfere in ways that might weaken family solidarity. However, he thinks that the decisions that Jason's father has made regarding his son's education are harmful. He is trying to decide if that justifies his responding to the Park family differently from the way in which he would generally respond to other families.

These four secondary principles can be useful in ethical reasoning in several ways. They elaborate what respect for persons entails, clarify the definition of an ethical problem, and provide some framework for thinking about ethical obligations. However, interpreting each principle in a specific situation requires careful thought. When applied, principles can conflict with one another. A situation may occur where it appears that acting in someone's best interest will require using deception or restricting freedom. An individual may have to decide which principles should be given priority in such cases. Sometimes establishing ethical priorities is easy. For example, reporting a person who has brutally beaten a child will probably lead to the restriction of the abuser's freedom, but this consequence is clearly justified. Concern for the child's interests, physical safety, and emotional well-being obviously take precedence over concern for the abuser's liberty. However, difficult cases abound. Here are some tough questions that stem from two of the cases:

1. Should Ms. Larkin allow Maria the freedom to make her own decision about whether to tell her parents about her pregnancy, or should she put pressure on her to share the news with them in the hope that support will be forthcoming?
2. Should Mr. Thompson allow Mr. Park the freedom to raise his son as he sees fit, or should he intervene because he believes that the unrelenting educational program the father has inflicted on his son is not in the boy's best interest?

Case-Specific Ethical Rules

We have been looking at how ethical principles are used to analyze problems and identify obligations. The reasoning pattern moved from the top down—from the most general principles to specific obligations.

However, it is often useful to abandon this pattern temporarily and approach the problem from the other direction. This entails a careful review of the facts of the case to try to determine just what is at issue, and an exploration of one's first intuitions about appropriate responses. Through this process, it is possible to generate case-specific rules that can be useful both in seeing an ethical problem more clearly and in examining the justification of various responses to it. These need not be stated in formal language—just as a list of ethical "shoulds" and "should nots" for counselors. To provide examples of case-specific rules, we can use the cases introduced in Chapters 1 and 3.

Ethical Rules in the Case of Maria

1. Be aware of all of the local agencies that provide help for pregnant teens.
2. Do everything you reasonably can to make sure that pregnant students have a good support system.
3. Know your legal obligations to students and their parents in regard to providing and withholding information about birth control, pregnancy, and abortion.
4. Do not impose your own views about sex and abortion on clients.
5. Help clients come to their own decisions about what to do.
6. Do everything you reasonably can to deter clients from harming themselves.
7. Work with parents to help children with serious problems.
8. Help students to see their situations clearly and avoid self-deception.

Ethical Rules in the Case of Jason

1. Do everything you reasonably can to prevent harm to students.
2. Be aware of and respect the values of the various cultural groups represented in the school.
3. Recognize the level of maturity of the students with whom you work, but also help them to participate to the fullest extent possible in addressing problems and determining possible solutions.
4. Work closely with parents to solve the problems of students.

Note how these rules help to locate the ethical issue in each case. Those relating to Maria's situation suggest that a counselor should both allow clients to make their own decisions and prevent them from doing harm to themselves. The problem is that one of Maria's decisions may be harmful to her. The counselor must assess the possible harm and determine if some intervention is justified. The rules relating to Jason's case suggest that the counselor should both prevent harm from befalling students and respect the child-rearing practices of parents. Mr. Thompson must determine if Mr. Park's approach is harmful enough to warrant his mediation.

Of course, one cannot accept any sort of case-specific ethical rule as valid without careful examination. A first step would be to see if it can be logically linked to the higher-order principles discussed earlier. But even in these two simple lists, there are problems. For example, in the case of Maria, agencies that deal with pregnancies are not value-neutral operations and, therefore, to refer Maria to one of them is a decision fraught with the value questions that have appeared from the outset. Similarly, the rule that enjoins us "to respect the values of the various cultural groups represented in the school" ought not to be accepted uncritically. Finally, we have directed counselors to do all they can to prevent harm (such as drug abuse or suicide) to students, as if this concept were not problematic in many contexts.

IDENTIFYING ALTERNATIVES AND THEIR LIKELY CONSEQUENCES

In the two cases we have been discussing, the counselors do considerable conjecturing about the outcomes of various options. For example, Ms. Larkin considers what would likely happen if she discloses the pregnancy to Maria's parents, and Mr. Thompson examines the likely consequences of calling a child protection agency. Conjecturing is essential in analyzing an ethical problem because it helps identify a full range of reasonable options and determine their likely consequences. Of course, this process has limits. An individual may be compelled to make a decision quickly without time for much reflection. Also, lacking omniscience, one may not be able to identify all of the choices or to be certain that actions will have anticipated results. However, these limitations do not mean that this kind of conjecturing is futile. Identifying options and likely consequences is the way to acquire as much control over outcomes as possible. By contrast, acting on impulse, trusting to luck, or dogmatically obeying a rule would be much more hazardous and irresponsible.

In Chapter 3, it was suggested that a problem connected with the consequentialist approach to ethical analysis is the difficulty of assessing the relative merits of various choices. For example, Ms. Larkin and

Mr. Thompson might be able to identify quite clearly what will be the results of the different approaches they might take, but the consequentialists are not very helpful when it comes to deciding which sets of outcomes are ethically more justified. This challenge can only be met by analyzing the outcomes on the basis of ethical principles. Once a counselor has done everything possible to identify reasonable alternatives for dealing with an ethical problem and the likely results, it must be determined which is most satisfactorily justified on the basis of the higher-order principles.

JUSTIFYING ETHICAL PRINCIPLES

As we have noted, sometimes moral principles conflict. For example, counselors may wonder if they should break confidentiality in order to comply with another important principle, such as protecting someone from harm. It is sometimes quite easy for counselors to determine which is the more important ethical principle. If it is a counselor's best professional judgment that a client truly intends to kill his girlfriend (as in the Tarasoff case reported in *Tarasoff v. Regents of the University of California*), it is more important to help the girlfriend protect her life than it is to maintain confidentiality. It seems difficult to imagine a convincing argument to show the reverse. More commonly, however, situations arise in which such clear-cut ethical judgments cannot be made. Cases occur in which the ethical arguments for maintaining and breaking confidentiality initially appear to be more or less equally important. It then becomes important for the counselor to weigh the "pluses" and "minuses" on each side in order to judge which course of action is more ethically justified. (See the discussion of Green's analysis of judging in Chapter 1.)

To assess the ethical importance of keeping client disclosures confidential, it is necessary to explore rather exactly just what justifies the claim that counselors do, in fact, have this obligation. In effect, the question is that of the skeptic who asks why confidentiality is an important issue in counseling. The argument must rely, in part, on higher order moral principles. Valuable insight is gained into just how important this practice is, which will, in turn, help reveal how much "ethical weight" to give it when it is compared with other counseling principles with which it may be in conflict.

It is interesting to note that the confidentiality rule is widely referred to as the "therapeutic promise": Counselors promise their clients (either explicitly or implicitly) that they will not disclose to others what transpires in their counseling sessions. Hence, if a counselor does disclose something said by a client, the ethical rule that "people ought to keep their promises" is being broken. Therefore, one reason for maintaining confidentiality is that counselors are expected to follow this precept.

However, suppose our skeptic is persistent and asks why one's promises should be kept. At this point, we need to further pursue this deontological line of argument and rest our justification on a higher ethical principle. It is the case that, when we make a promise, we are obliged to do whatever it is that we promised. When counselors promise confidentiality to clients, they obligate themselves not to tell what the client discloses in counseling sessions. Any counselor who promises to maintain confidentiality, with no intention of doing so, is not making a promise at all but simply lying to the client. A promise must be truthful. A "lying promise" is a contradiction in terms. Thus, our ethical principle of promise keeping is justified by a higher ethical principle—respect for truth.

Furthermore, commitment to truth is grounded in the principle of respect for persons. Questioning this principle is tantamount to asking "Why should I be moral?" or "Why should I be rational about human conduct?" Such a question implies a contradiction, for it presupposes the value of rationality—that the counselor should respect evidence, care about logic, and take clients and their questions seriously—while the whole rational enterprise is in doubt.

The fact that a breach of confidence violates a client's right to privacy gives rise to a second line of justification—this time of a consequentialist kind. Protecting privacy is not the same as maintaining confidentiality because the latter extends its secrecy to many things that are not, in fact, private. Yet, the two principles have a common purpose—they enable individuals to control the spread of information about themselves. It is easy to see that when counselors maintain confidentiality, they are furthering their clients' freedom to keep control of personal information. If confidentiality is not maintained, clients lose privacy and may be unable to protect themselves from harm.

The third justification is also of a consequentialist nature. It is common for clients to disclose to counselors things that are innermost to them—shameful personal secrets may be disclosed that leave them vulnerable. It is essential for clients to be able to trust their counselors, to be assured that their advisors will not hurt them by disclosing personal information and will use it only to help them deal with their problems. Building trust is centrally important to a counseling relationship or therapeutic alliance that is, in turn, essential for progress. It is, then, the client's interest in making progress that further justifies the claim that counselors do, in fact, have an ethical obligation to maintain confidentiality.

Three strong arguments to justify this principle have been produced. However, several points need reiterating. First, we are now in a good position to see just how important the principle of confidentiality is from an ethical point of view. It is clear, for example, that a number of very important ethical principles are violated whenever confidentiality is broken. The client's freedom to control personal information is diminished, the counselor's promise to the client has been broken, and the bond of trust that is so important for the client's progress is likely to have been dealt a serious blow. Note that while violating any one of these principles would be a serious transgression, the gravity of the situation is most apparent when "ethical damage" has been done in all three categories.

Second, we are in a much better position to make a sound judgment when, in some specific case, there are ethical reasons to believe that confidentiality ought to be broken. Suppose, for example, that justification for maintaining confidentiality was based solely on a promise to clients not to disclose what transpires in counseling sessions. Although promise keeping is surely a very important ethical obligation, it is not difficult to see reasons that, in some circumstances, it is justifiable to override our commitment to keep our promises in favor of serving other concerns. However, because we can now understand better that breaking confidentiality involves other serious ethical breaches, it will require a much stronger justification to warrant a judgment to do so.

When one speaks of "weighing" the merits of each side of an ethical problem, it is apparent that there are ethical reasons for two incompatible actions. This process of producing full justification for each option helps clarify the "weighing" metaphor. Of course, the procedure will not be so neat and tidy that one can merely count the justifications for the alternatives and choose the action with the higher number. But in developing all of the arguments for an ethical position to the fullest, we are in the best position to appraise its importance.

SUMMARY

This set of basic principles is necessary for reasoning about one's ethical obligations. Respect for persons is the fundamental ethical principle and is logically connected to four second-order *prima facie* principles: considering the interests of others, maximizing freedom, respecting truth, and treating persons equally. As the case studies illustrate, these principles could illuminate ethical problems faced by school counselors.

When one brings the higher-order principles to bear on an ethical problem, one is reasoning from the top down—from the most fundamental and general principles to the identification of one's ethical obligations in a specific situation. However, it can also be useful to reason from the specific to the general—for example, by identifying the ethical obligations in a given situation and determining if they can be justified by connecting them with the higher-order principles.

An analysis of alternatives for action and their likely consequences can contribute to the resolution of ethical problems. The justification of ethical principles has also been established so that their importance can be compared to that of other fundamental assumptions in a concrete case.

There is no step-by-step procedure for thinking through ethical problems. The task is too complex to be amenable to a recipe. It is better for the counselor to use a variety of approaches, such as the following:

- Consider how each of the fundamental principles might apply to the problem and what obligations they suggest.
- Formulate a set of case-specific ethical principles that seem implicit in the situation without extensive analysis.
- Identify the options available and the likely consequences; develop the best ethical justification possible for the most promising; try to establish which alternative is most justified.

These phases of problem resolution may be started independently of each other, but if the counselor has tenacity and some good fortune, they should converge.

CHAPTER 5

Ethical Principles and Concepts

Chapter 4 introduced a schema of moral reasoning to help counselors deliberate about ethical problems. However, such analysis requires a sound grasp of the principles and associated concepts at the core of the framework. A more detailed treatment of the principles will show how they form the basis for ethical problems and offer guidance toward their resolution. However, one characteristic of this form of reasoning is troublesome. The principles of freedom, consideration of interests, equality, and truth are sufficiently general that they sometimes generate different—even conflicting—conclusions. Counselors are familiar with this situation. In fact, we all must live with the moral condition, part of which involves recognizing the force and the limitations of moral reasoning. In this chapter, each of these principles is explored to show how they structure—indeed, "create"—ethical problems in school counseling. This chapter also acknowledges that there are situations where no principle can be applied with precision and certainty.

CONSIDERATION OF INTERESTS

Chapter 4 claims that the second-order principle of consideration of interests stems from the first-order principle of respect for persons. This obligates us to recognize that all persons—including ourselves—have needs, problems, desires, goals, and life plans. Like respect for persons, consideration of interests is both a self- and other-regarding principle; that is, our needs and those of others have moral status when we are deciding what we ought to do. In one sense, this principle is stronger than "negative freedom" (Berlin, 1969), which would require us simply to make space for persons to pursue their own goals. Here we are required to consider positively—all things being equal—ways in which to further the designs of others, especially where we have made a commitment to them as their parents, teachers, and counselors.

Thus, school counselors must be more than just good listeners. They should be actively involved in the task of determining what the needs of students are and how they can be met. This does not mean that they should impose their own values on students nor give approval and encouragement to any and all plans proposed by their clients. School counselors have the dual role of helping others to identify and achieve what they want out of life and doing what they reasonably can to protect their clients' interests when they are threatened by outside forces or by their own lack of good judgment.

When Interests Collide

A school counselor is likely to experience two kinds of ethical problems relating to this principle. In working with a client, a counselor may discover that the student's parents or teachers also have legitimate interests that must be carefully considered. The situation can be volatile if a conflict arises between the interests as perceived by the client and as seen by other parties. Even though a counselor's overriding concern is the welfare of his or her clients, ethically the legitimate interests of others cannot be ignored. That is, this principle extends to all persons, and even parents and teachers are persons, despite the denials of some distraught adolescents.

Of course, a counselor can try to avert an ethical dilemma by helping clients see how others will be affected by their actions and trying to persuade them to take into account the interests of important people in their lives when deciding what to do (see the discussion of Maria's case in Chapter 1 and Jennifer's in Chapter 7). At times, counselors must be moral educators, and reorientating clients to the moral geography of their world is a legitimate part of the role. Because the notion of interests is necessarily value laden, and the people involved are—from the moral point of view—persons, these discussions are unavoidably normative.

However, this strategy may fail, and the counselor may have no alternative but to weigh the interests of the client against those of other parties, determine which have higher priority, and act to protect them. If the counselor determines that the interests of others are more compelling, it may be necessary to oppose those advanced by the client.

When Assessments Clash

A similar problem occurs when counselors discover that their appraisal of a client's best interests is in conflict with the client's own assessment. In Chapter 4, we pointed out that the concept of "interest" is ambiguous. If we are trying to establish the interests of persons, we can ask them what they are "interested in," or ask what they think is "in their best interest." Often, a client's answers to these questions will coincide. About the former, the client is the authority, so to speak, because this sense of interest is determined by first-person, psychological reports. Because the latter involves a value judgment, overriding, first-person authority is eroded; someone else may know better what is in your best interest, whether by greater experience, knowledge, or insight. Often, answers to the first question are relevant to answering the second because they can provide valuable material for consideration. But it is equally clear that these two lines of inquiry could result in different, even conflicting, conclusions. No doubt, conscientious counselors use both strategies in the process of assessing their clients' concerns.

The second dimension to the application of the interests principle concerns the means advanced to promote interests. The counselor and the client may agree on the ends to be pursued, but disagree over the means to achieve them. Here, norms such as risk, efficiency, and the appraisal of the multiple consequences of an action come into play.

In discussions about interests, the truth principle plays a supporting role. Both parties should be aiming to discover what a client's true interests are and the rational means to achieve them. Fantasy, ignorance, prejudice, and immaturity are obstacles that may have to be overcome. Clients may be under considerable stress, or lack self-esteem and confidence. Crises may be so overwhelming that clients are unable to think clearly and might decide that, to protect their interests, drastic courses of action are required, such as quitting school, running away from home, or submitting to an abusive boyfriend.

As clients describe their problems and what they see as their most promising options, counselors begin to form their own questions and judgments. Does the client show signs of abuse, fatigue, or lack of nourishment? Is the client's description of the situation coherent? Is it likely that a more serious problem is hiding behind the "presenting problem"? Does the client's plan for dealing with the dilemma indicate a good grasp of reality?

Sometimes, counselors find that their assessment of a client's interests is in conflict with the client's. Counseling theories offer various strategies for how to proceed in such circumstances, though most advise that, in the first instance, the counselor should try to avoid open confrontation by reframing the problem and raising questions (all of which invoke a moral dimension) to help the client reevaluate the situation: What goals is the client pursuing? What are the likely short- and long-term results of the actions being considered? What are the risks? Are there other ways to deal with the problem that might be more promising? What conception of the "good life" underlies the discussion? What value priorities are at work? By discussing questions like these, the counselor may succeed in clarifying the client's interests. And perhaps the counselor's assessment must be revised. But, if the two views remain unreconciled, the counselor may be inclined to take a more direct approach. This may involve disclosing a personal view, warning the client about the dangers inherent in the client's current plans, or giving reasons why another course of action is more likely to protect or promote the client's interests. If this strategy also fails, the counselor will have to consider taking some direct action that the client may see as a violation of the freedom principle. For example, the counselor may decide to inform the student's parents about a stated intention to run away or call the social services department to initiate an investigation of the student's family. Such actions may be interpreted as unjustified paternalism and may very well have a devastating effect on the counselor-client relationship. A counselor considering such action should be very sure—both on moral and professional/prudential grounds—that the interpretation of the client's interests is accurate and that the action is justified in spite of the risks.

There are many situations that could present a school counselor with ethical problems related to the consideration of interests principle. Consider how a counselor might respond to Cases Eighteen and Nineteen in Chapter 8.

MAXIMIZING FREEDOM

In Chapter 4, it was argued that some kinds of freedom are required by respect for persons, thereby making room, in the most general way, for persons to be rationally self-determining. If there were no freedoms, it would be impossible to decide upon one's own goals and the avenues to reach them. The complete absence of freedom is at the heart of fascism, a state that is powerfully depicted in literature in Huxley's *Brave New World* and in philosophy in Plato's *Republic*. In such societies, no one (except, of course, the authorities) is trusted to make any—or, at least, any important—decisions about the course of his or her own life.

Because such systematic repression of autonomy and, thus, human dignity is repugnant to most, it is no wonder that "freedom" is so susceptible to being used as a slogan. The word can easily serve as a rhetorical banner to rally people to different—and sometimes conflicting—

causes. Because the concept of freedom is subject to many interpretations, people can appear to agree about the need to promote it while disagreeing on the actions and policies required. For example, some groups believe that to increase our freedom we need to decrease governmental regulation of our economic and social life, whereas others believe that it would require an increase in governmental intervention in social and economic institutions to provide more equality and, thus, more freedom of opportunity for disadvantaged groups.

When people recommend an increase in freedom, it is important to clarify what sort of freedom they are talking about and to show the connections between their conception of freedom and the means they are advocating to realize it. Counseling theories are not immune to these general points. All counselors might agree that we should promote our clients' freedom but, because we adhere to different psychological theories, we disagree about what this entails.

As a moral matter, what is it reasonable to expect a school counselor to do to "maximize the freedom" of clients? Although the focus is on personal freedom, it will become clear that some of what falls under this category is related to other kinds of freedom, such as political and economic freedom.

The concept of freedom that seems most appropriate for our purposes has to do with a person's ability to make rational choices, to act upon them, and to gain the intended benefits. What sorts of things interfere with a person's freedom interpreted in this way?

Internal Constraints

It is useful to distinguish between internal and external constraints, even if, in some areas, the distinction is blurred. Internal constraints can be further categorized as either epistemological (having to do with knowledge) or psychological.

Epistemological constraints. When faced with a problem, students may simply be ignorant of some facts or misinformed about other facts. In either case, their capacity to promote their own best interests may be jeopardized. The remedy in this case is simple—supply them with the relevant information. For example, they may not know, or may be mistaken about, the entrance requirements for college and, thus, may need to be led through the application process.

Other cases are not so straightforward. Students may have very limited horizons when it comes to thinking about postsecondary education. They may know about admissions standards but not appreciate the value of higher education and are unable to "see themselves on campus." The task of expanding students' vistas requires providing them with information plus some positive experience that will change their attitudes. The counselor may need to sponsor student visits to college campuses or arrange for university students to return to their former school to talk with classes.

More difficult still is the victim of, say, a sexist view of the world. Imagine a bright female student who declines to apply to college because what she thinks she might gain there is not part of her conception of her role. This young person may have collected all the information, visited campuses, and talked with university students, but she lacks a framework within which to give the option fair, rational consideration. What weighs against her is a limited conception of what she might become. As she says of herself, "I'm just a girl." She has learned this view from those around her and has found plenty of support for it. The remedy for this restriction on freedom might be a difficult and controversial form of education known as "consciousness raising."

It is to Freud's credit that he saw that education could alleviate some restrictions on rational action. His view of the scope and sources of that education was unfortunately narrow. Although he was prepared to look at family history, he was not willing to examine critically family structure or other structural features of society. Radical psychological theory has focused on such elements, and claims that much distortion of judgment and, consequently, of emotions is the direct result of living in dysfunctional institutions, including—some would say, especially—the family, church, and school. Inappropriate behavior is seen as a response to a society in conflict. Both the society and such response to it need to be changed if clients' freedom is to be maximized. The first task is to understand the sources of discontent, then to change the behavior, and, perhaps, work to reform harmful institutions and the laws and policies that support them. Radical counseling focuses on institutions (and their vested interests) as the source of problems rather than isolating the individual. The radical counselor takes risks, for this kind of work may not be viewed as politically correct.

Psychological restraints. A person's freedom is curtailed by compulsions and addictions. Repressed emotions, say, from past sexual abuse, restrict or distort present relationships. Other limitations are related more to personality traits such as extreme cowardice or timidity that prevent a person from acting freely. Low self-esteem, weakness of will, and low motivation often interfere with doing what one knows one ought to do. Depression can crush the ability to act. Some people's freedom is choked because they fail to perform to the level of their ability when under the slightest pressure. This list could be extended to great length, but these examples indicate something of the range of conditions that could limit choices or the ability to act on them.

External Constraints

Some limitations are primarily external to the person. A person's choice-making will be affected by social, cultural, economic, and political factors. Not everyone is free to attend an Ivy League university because the tuition may be beyond the resources of many. Those whose English is poor, whether or not it is a second language, may find this a professional barrier. Racial and other kinds of prejudice may interfere with educational and business progress. Women may find "invisible ceilings" at work and experience the "double-bind" at home. The extent of the damage done by sexual harassment is only now being acknowledged.

Some of these constraints are within an individual's power to remedy; other restrictions rest in a wider political domain and require policy and attitude changes. At some times, political action is called for (such as civil rights protests); at other times, public education is needed (as in campaigns to promote awareness of the needs of those with disabilities); and sometimes litigation seems to be the only route available (as in court challenges over sexual harassment or school placements).

Interpreting the Freedom Principle

These examples open a vast arena of possibilities to maximize a person's freedom. Using the negative principle, maximizing freedom would require a *prima facie* obligation to refrain from imposing restrictions on the choices and actions of other persons and from interfering with their deliberations about what choices to make or their ability to act on them. This can be described as the liberal position. From this perspective, coercion, manipulation, and indoctrination would be examples of interference with a person's freedom.

The positive and more radical interpretation calls for us to maximize the freedom of persons by helping them understand and overcome both the external conditions and the personal characteristics that are limiting their choices and actions. This means helping the client to understand the circumstances that constrain freedom (whether these are political, social economic, or psychological); deliberate more thoroughly and rationally about the options available; and develop a strategy to tackle the situation, including as a goal the overcoming of personal problems that restrict the client's ability to deliberate about choices or act upon them. Constraints to freedom that are political, social, or economic would call for exploring with the client appropriate forums for social action; those that are strictly psychological would require ensuring that appropriate treatment is available.

All of these ways of maximizing freedom are things that school counselors do routinely. However, it may be helpful to list some specific counseling actions and the circumstances in which the actions could be justified as ways of maximizing the freedom of a client.

Counseling Strategies Under Particular Circumstances

1. *Noninterference*: Let us imagine that a male client is mature and intellectually capable. He discusses a problem with the counselor and determines what he wants to do. The counselor may not think it is the best plan of action but recognizes that the client understands both the problem and several alternatives for dealing with it, as well as the risks associated with the choice he has made. The principle of maximizing freedom means, minimally, refraining from any action that would constitute interference with the implementation of the client's plan. The counselor should not manipulate or coerce the client to abandon his plan for another that the counselor believes is better.
2. *Providing information*: In this instance, a female client is having a difficult time making a decision about universities because she lacks important, relevant information. The counselor should be able to provide it or to identify appropriate sources. Counselors, then, are professionally obligated to be well informed about such resources.
3. *Assessing options*: A client is aware of the reasonable alternatives for dealing with a problem but is having difficulty deciding which holds the most promise. The counselor can help the client identify the probable short- and long-term consequences of various options (in particular, how each contributes to the expansion of freedom) and the values that are implicit in each. The counselor can also help the client to clarify his or her feelings about the likely results.
4. *Helping the client acquire needed abilities*: The client has a reasonable plan to deal with the problem but is lacking some necessary ability or attribute to carry it out. These can vary from the specific academic skills involved in improving reading, study, or

the writing of papers; to social matters, such as one's presentation at a job interview; to general human development, such as the need for a broad, liberal education. The counselor can help the client develop these capacities directly or assist the client to enter a program that provides them.

5. *Bolstering confidence and initiative*: The client has a reasonable plan to deal with the problem but lacks the confidence to implement it. The counselor can work on the improvement of the client's self-esteem and offer encouragement.
6. *Deterring self-destructive action*: The client has indicated an intention to do something rash or self-destructive that would reduce his or her future freedom. The counselor would be justified in intervening to help the client overcome this shortsightedness and see the impending danger.

It might be concluded from this list of strategies that it is the school counselor's role to give whatever kind of assistance is needed to enable students to make their own decisions. This might be true if the freedom principle were absolute, but it is, instead, only a second-order principle that directs us when all other things are thought to be equal. Often, other considerations outweigh the obligation to maximize or respect the freedom of the client. Thus, the counselor may never need to take direct action to influence a client's decisions, such as forcing, coercing, manipulating, or interfering with the implementation of the client's choices after they are made. These sorts of actions would put the maximizing freedom principle at risk, although, in some dire circumstances, it might be moral to sacrifice this principle for another principle. However, there is nothing in the freedom principle that prevents a counselor from influencing decisions, say, by giving advice. At times, clients need to hear an adult voice even if they do not act on the advice at the time. Only those in the grip of an extreme, nondirective counseling theory would think otherwise. The mistake made in such theories is to promote a version of the freedom principle as absolute.

Operating under the freedom principle presupposes that the counselor is in essential agreement with the client about the interests to be pursued and the means to be employed. A counselor who has a very strong spiritual value orientation would have difficulty counseling a student whose only motive for any action is material gain—at least when all that the student is seeking is the promotion of such limited goals. Imagine for a moment that the counselor has no qualms about promoting the get-rich dreams of students but that the route a female student has chosen is prostitution. Having seen the film *Pretty Woman*, she thinks that using her body is the best way to "make a million." First, the glamorized version of the life of prostitutes needs scrutiny under the truth principle. But, second, let us suppose that millions are there for the making; there is the moral matter of whether one should allow oneself to be used solely to satisfy someone else's desires. Under the freedom principle, a counselor has an obligation not to promote the readiness of a client for such a life, but instead to engage in moral education as an antidote.

The ethical problems related to this principle stem from the fact that clients are not always capable of making responsible choices. Clients may lack the necessary maturity or be so overwhelmed by the problems that they are in a state of what may be called "reduced rationality." If a person is incapable of seeing available alternatives and their implications, it seems inappropriate to say that the actions they took resulted from "free choices." Clearly, in some situations, a counselor is ethically justified in interfering with a student's plans. For example, if a client wishes to solve a problem in a manner that is clearly self-destructive or will seriously harm another, noninterference could make the counselor both ethically and legally culpable.

The difficulty of interpreting the freedom principle in counseling cases is in determining whether or not the persons in the situation are capable of making responsible (including moral) choices. If they are, the principle suggests that the counselor's role should be limited to the kinds of assistance in problem solving described above. Unfortunately, it is often difficult for a counselor to ascertain the extent to which clients are capable of making such decisions. It is also difficult to know if clients really intend to take the rash actions they sometimes talk about in a counseling session. Hence, it is often difficult for a counselor to judge if some active intervention is needed and, if it is, what kind is appropriate. Of course, laws, codes of ethics, and, often, school board policies specify the conditions under which the school counselor should actively intervene. However, these guidelines usually cover only extreme cases, as when a client has threatened suicide or serious harm to someone else. The counselor may have to make an on-the-spot, personal decision in a less grave case.

One of the difficulties involved is that opinions vary greatly regarding the capacities of individuals to take responsible action. The following hypothetical statements of counselors—admittedly representing extreme attitudes—make it clear how differently the issue of the client's responsibility can be viewed:

- It is easy for me to tell when my clients are capable of acting responsibly regarding their own welfare. It is when they are able to see that my interpretation of their problems and my ideas for dealing with them are the correct ones. When that happens, I know they are ready to manage their own lives without interference.

- Students are children until they reach the legal age for adulthood. Their welfare until then is primarily the responsibility of their parents. However, at school, it is school officials who must determine what is best for them. Children are in no position to decide what is good for themselves. Of course, it is appropriate for them to share their problems and concerns with their parents, teachers, and counselors, but not to decide what actions are best for their own welfare.
- Everyone—even a young child or an adolescent with serious problems—has an intuitive sense of what is good and bad for them. Unless children are very young or have a serious psychological dysfunction, they are capable of making virtually all of the important decisions regarding their own welfare. School personnel should not impose on students their own views of what is good for them, and they should do what they can to deter parents from doing so.

Each of these positions may have merit in some circumstances, but each has problems that could result in serious damage to human lives if applied universally. Determining just how much freedom of choice and action for the student is optimal in counseling and what kinds of interventions are ethically justified are problems that every counselor faces regularly. Consider the situations described in Cases Eight, Nine, and Ten in Chapter 8, in light of this discussion of the freedom principle.

RESPECT FOR TRUTH

In Chapter 4, the obvious connection between the principles of respect for truth and respect for persons is noted. Intentionally deceiving someone, under most circumstances, would be a clear indication of lack of respect because it prevents that person from making decisions on a rational basis. The principle obligates us to assess situations clearly, and, when appropriate, to report what we see accurately and respect the rules of evidence and logic in giving reasons and weighing the reasoning of others.

Like the freedom principle, respect for truth possesses both a negative and positive requirement. To avoid deceiving others is the negative obligation. This interpretation requires simply that we not lie to others and, presumably, to ourselves (we do have an obligation to try to avoid self-deception).

The positive interpretation necessitates our seeking information actively about all matters, including the effects of our actions on others. From the moral point of view, counselors and clients alike cannot assess actions solely on the basis of how well they provide for their own needs and desires. Counselors feel obligated to assist students in acquiring the information they need or interpreting what is available to help them make intelligent choices. Helping students assess promotional material from postsecondary institutions or employment advertisements is a useful service that falls under the truth principle.

Facing the Truth

In personal counseling sessions, clients may find that facing the truth is very painful and, thus, may be inclined to distort reality to protect themselves from exposure. Counselors frequently must probe tortured psyches to help uncover truths that must be faced if a life is to be righted. Clients may be wedded to their prejudices, resentments, actions, or addictions. An alcoholic's capacity for denying the truth is universal. A trusting relationship may be the key, but savvy on the part of the counselor may also be critical to unlocking deeply held secrets.

Counselors must be aware of ways in which they too can tumble into untruth. They can be myopic if overly committed to a specific school of thought. For example, they might adhere to a theory of family dynamics so that everything that is offered by a client is interpreted in that particular light and more is actively sought to confirm the picture and the theory. The resulting distortion can be disastrous for the client and family. Counselors may apply prejudices and stereotypes to individuals with harmful consequences. Finally, counselors may unconsciously begin to tailor their own conceptions to fit their community's views of what is "politically correct." In this case, truth may become a casualty.

Honesty versus Transparency

One possible misinterpretation of respect for truth needs to be noted. Although the principle clearly requires honesty in our dealings with others, it does not mandate that either the counselor or the client be totally open with the other. Honesty and transparency ought not to be confused. Psychologists such as Rogers (1961, 1980) and Maslow (1968, 1970) argue for the need for open, intimate relationships, but this can be achieved without revealing all of one's thoughts about mutual acquaintances and experiences. In some situations, not disclosing one's thoughts or feelings is justified as a simple act of kindness. In other situations, personal revelations might be counterproductive to the goals of counseling or irrelevant to the issue being explored. In still other situations, sharing something with a client might be a clear violation of high-level, ethical obligations—as, for example, when a counselor has an obligation to keep the contents of other counseling sessions confidential. The principle of respect for truth is not a license for voyeurism on the part of the counselor or compulsive transparency on the part of the client.

Counselors' specific ethical obligations related to the respect for truth principle require them to do the following:

1. Make an effort to assess their own abilities and limits accurately and, thus, reduce the chances of self-deception; recognize the possibility of bias; and be willing to make referrals to other professionals in situations where they lack training or experience.
2. Seek all relevant information and check its reliability before taking any action that will significantly affect the life of a client or the lives of others.
3. Maintain intellectual integrity when working with clients, colleagues, and others. Counselors should present information as accurately as possible, offer opinions and arguments objectively, and keep an open mind to the views of others. In all ordinary circumstances, they should keep promises.
4. Do everything they reasonably can to help clients make a realistic appraisal of their situation and plans for improving it. This means, for example, that counselors should not contribute to the self-deception of a client and should help clients appreciate the possible hazards in a proposal.
5. Take steps to ensure that clients and others do not misinterpret what they say or do.

Acting in accordance with the respect for truth principle entails avoiding deception, promoting a true view of the world as far as one can ascertain it, acquiring relevant and accurate information before taking actions that are likely to affect others, and helping others to see the truth about matters of importance to their welfare. These seem like reasonable guidelines for counselors (and everyone else, for that matter), but sometimes following them is difficult in practice. Consider how you think a school counselor should respond to the situations described in Cases One, Two, and Four of Chapter 8, keeping in mind the respect for truth principle as we have explored it here.

EQUALITY

Like freedom, equality is a complex concept and is often used as a slogan. Also, like freedom, it is a concept that is easier to clarify from a negative angle. Let us consider some situations in which a person's actions are apparently in clear violation of the equality principle:

1. An employer decides that he ought to promote one of his workers to a supervisory post but considers only his male employees for the position.
2. An athletic coach selects members of a varsity athletic team on the basis of grade point average (GPA).
3. A mother and father throw an extravagant birthday for their young daughter and later ignore the birthday of their young son.

It is not difficult to recognize the injustice in such situations. Even little children seem to sense that something is wrong when someone else is given preferential treatment over them for no apparent reason. The little boy in the third case would likely protest and demand an explanation: "That isn't fair! Why does Susie get a party, presents, and everything, and I get nothing?"

The paradigm case of inequality is a situation in which a number of individuals are in the same or similar circumstances, yet some are treated better or worse than the others without good moral reasons to justify the differential treatment. The equality principle obligates us to treat everyone in similar situations in the same way unless there are relevant differences in the persons or the circumstances that justify differential treatment. The difficulties in applying the principle are those of establishing what specific differences in persons and situations are sufficient and relevant to justify differential treatment and determining what kinds of differential treatment are justified.

Theories of justice have always jousted over the appropriate criteria for justifying the unequal distribution of desirable goods (see Rawls,1971, for a contemporary example). In most Western countries, we have reached a consensus that some criteria that were used in the past, like bloodline and social position, are unjust for apportioning basic education and health services. Much controversy still surrounds other criteria such as gender and racial issues. We are familiar with strong arguments over questions like the following: Should women be assigned to combat roles in our armed forces? Should gay and lesbian people be admitted to the military? If there are a number of equally qualified applicants for a job, is it always right to give it to the applicant from a minority group? If only a few places are available in a law school, is it ever right to offer them to minority persons even though they are less qualified than those from the majority? School counselors, like everyone else, are not immune to challenges to standard applications of the equality principle.

When we are in situations in which decisions have to be made about the fair treatment of a number of individuals, the best way to begin is to assume that one is obligated to treat everyone in exactly the same manner. Then, if it appears that acting in this way would be unjust, we need to consider what makes the plan ethically unsatisfactory, what differential treatment of individuals would be ethically more defensible, and how the new plan could be justified.

Let us return briefly to the three examples of injustice offered at the beginning of this section to see how this strategy might be employed. In each of the cases, there may be good reasons for not treating the individuals involved in an identical manner, but no apparent justification for the differential treatment given to the individuals. The employer could probably develop a good argument for using ability as the chief criterion for selecting employees for promotion, but it is hard to imagine a convincing argument for using gender as the criterion. Similarly, demonstrated ability would seem to be the justified key criterion for a coach to use in selecting varsity team players. The coach may be able to develop an argument for using some minimum grade point average as a requirement for participating in interscholastic sports, but it is hard to see how a GPA could be justified as the deciding factor in picking varsity team members. The parents in the third case seem clearly unjust in providing a gala birthday party for their daughter but not for their son. It may appear that the equality principle obligates them to treat the two children in an identical manner on the occasion of their birthday, but note that some differences in treatment could be quite easily justified. For example, suppose the girl loves social gatherings and the boy dislikes them, or the girl loves skating and the boy does not. Clearly, the parents are justified in selecting gifts on the basis of what they think each of the children would enjoy. They are not obligated to give identical gifts to each. If there is a significant separation in the ages of the children, other differences in treatment (such as the length of the party and the kind of activities and refreshments) could be justified. Equal or fair treatment, then, is not synonymous with identical treatment.

We can use this case to identify another kind of problem in applying the equality principle. Suppose the parents suffer a financial disaster between the two birthdays and are unable to give the boy, whose birthday comes later, the same kind of lavish party they gave the girl.

Their treatment of the two children would not be equitable, yet the parents are not acting unethically. People cannot reasonably be obligated to do things that are beyond their capacities.

Interpreting the Equality Principle

Let us now consider how the equality principle might apply to the role of the school counselor. *Prima facie*, it seems reasonable to expect a counselor to have equal concern for the educational progress and personal welfare of all of the students in the school and to provide services in an equitable manner. This does not mean that every student should be given equal counseling time or that all counseling clients should be treated in the same way—relevant differences among persons and situations must be considered in determining ethical obligations. We will have to consider what differences in treatment of students and parents are justified and how they are justified.

It is reasonable to expect school counselors to be available to provide certain services for all students and their parents in the school community. For example, they can provide information about the social services and training facilities available and the entrance requirements of various colleges. However, the situation at most schools makes it impossible for counselors to provide all the counseling services needed. Typically, a school has only a few counselors and hundreds of students who could benefit from working with them. This situation means that most school counselors share the same ethical problems: What is the most equitable way to distribute school counseling services? What differences among clients, and prospective clients, justify giving more time and attention to some over others?

Clearly, most school counselors cannot offer the full range of counseling services to all students. They must establish some criteria and priorities for determining who to work with and what kinds of services to render. Some possibilities, like "first come, first serve" or "by parental request," seem patently unacceptable from an ethical point of view, for they could result in the counselor working with clients with relatively minor problems, while those with serious problems receive no help at all. The equality principle obligates school counselors to allot their services on the basis of need.

Fortunately, many students can maintain their psychological and emotional well-being and achieve academic success in school with virtually no assistance from a counselor. However, it is not always obvious to parents, teachers, or even to students themselves, which students need counseling services. Although the academic records of students may be an indication of who is doing well and who is not, many apparently successful students are quietly suffering through some very severe problems like depression or child abuse.

Establishing a Hierarchy of Counseling Needs

Besides the problem of determining who should receive counseling services, school counselors often face another difficult ethical conundrum related to this principle. The equality principle obligates counselors to establish a basis for working with clients that will guide them consistently, regardless of who the client is. For example, if counselors maintained the confidentiality of counseling sessions for female clients but gossiped about male clients, they would be clearly violating the principle. However, counselors are obligated to recognize differences in the situations of clients that require them to be treated in different ways, according to their special needs. The ethical problem is establishing just what sorts of conditions justify a counselor in departing from established procedures and what kinds of special treatment are justified. We can illustrate this problem by returning to the case of Maria from Chapter 1.

Ms. Larkin was trying to decide if Maria's problems were serious enough to justify the cancellation of later appointments. If she decides that Maria's needs take precedence over the needs of other clients, she is assuming that the problems of those with later appointments are not as serious as Maria's. She needs to develop a justifiable hierarchy of counseling needs to guide her decisions about departures from normal routine. She would also be obligated to try to find a way to provide for the needs of those students who lose their opportunity to meet with her. Consider the implications of this discussion for the situations described in Cases Five and Six of Chapter 8. Do you think the facts of each case justify a departure from established procedures?

CHAPTER 6

Problems that "Go with the Territory"

In the preceding chapters, we have tried to clarify what ethical problems are and have offered strategies for dealing with them. Now we would like to identify the kinds of ethical problems school counselors and others in similar roles are most likely to encounter. In connection with each kind of problem, we will discuss how and why problems arise and offer some suggestions for dealing with them.

VALUE CONFLICTS

It is hard to imagine a school counselor surviving a day without experiencing ethical problems related to value conflicts. School counselors bring their own collection of personal values to every session with their clients. Without doubt, their educational backgrounds and life experiences have resulted in some well-formed value convictions about certain matters: What do children need? What is the appropriate role of parents in the life of a child? What constitutes a good educational program? How should teachers treat students? What are the best methods of classroom control and student discipline? What exactly is the role of the school counselor? What is the appropriate relationship between counselors and others who have roles in the school, such as students, parents, faculty, and administrators? Questions like these call for judgments about what is good, right, and desirable.

The students who come to counseling have views about what is worthwhile and how to pursue it, as do their parents and the teachers and administrators with whom counselors work. It should not be surprising if counselor and client have relevant but incompatible value convictions, conflicting ideas about what the problem is and what should be done about it, or even what role the counselor should play. The cases presented in Chapters 1 and 3 present examples of value conflicts.

Ms. Larkin thought it would be good to involve Maria's parents in the process; Maria disagreed. Mr. Thompson and Jason's father, Mr. Park, had very different views regarding what Jason's problems were and how to deal with them. Ms. White, the principal, also had a strong opinion about the best approach.

Some value conflicts in school counseling can be foreseen and prevented. When a counselor is considering whether to apply for or accept a school position, it is important to give thought to just what the job entails. What exactly are the duties? Is the job limited to academic and career counseling, or will there be some personal counseling, too? Where will the ultimate authority lie? Are requests by the principal always expected to be carried out, or will there be areas of personal autonomy? What sorts of information must be passed on to administrators, faculty, and parents? What information should be withheld? Some of these questions may be answered by reading the official job description, but it is likely to provide only a very general listing of the counselor's duties. For a clear picture of what will be expected and what kinds of decisions are for the counselor to make, frank discussion of these matters with the principal and others may be needed. Perhaps negotiation can resolve some of the issues. However, if a counselor's value convictions are incompatible with the values of administrators where application is being made, it might be wiser to look elsewhere for a job than to face the inevitable dilemmas that will occur later.

Another way a counselor can head off potential value conflicts is to establish clear counseling ground rules with both students and parents at the beginning of counselor-client relationships. Both students and their parents should be provided with at least some general information about what will occur in the counseling sessions, especially if the students are minors. Will the counseling be limited to school-related matters, or is any problem the client is experiencing an appropriate focus for counseling? What are the limits of confidentiality? If the client is the student, what sort of progress report, if any, will be passed on to parents and administrators? What, if anything, will the client's teachers be told about what is transpiring in the counseling sessions? If clients and their parents are provided with the ground rules the counselor will follow, the likelihood of serious conflicts later is reduced. Of course, it is possible to have so many standards, or to make them so stringent, that students will be frightened away or parents will refuse to grant permission for their children to see the counselor.

In spite of these efforts to avert value conflicts, it is probably inevitable that they will occur. Solutions to this kind of problem do not come easily. One strategy is to determine whose values should prevail in a given situation. From one perspective, the freedom principle demands that clients should have the final decision about what is in their own interests, but it could be argued that parents have the right to determine what is good for their children. Counselors might maintain that they have the most expertise for analyzing psychological and emotional problems and deciding what should be done about them. Each of these arguments has merit, but it would be dangerous to assume, before careful evaluation, that any one of those involved in a case has the clearest understanding of the problem and the best plan for dealing with it. Students can be wrong about what is or would be good for them, as can their parents. The counselor's view will be less than omniscient. Rather than trying to establish whose values should prevail, it seems wiser to consider a number of alternative views, regardless of the sources, and try to determine which course of action is most reasonable and most promising. Chapter 4 contains some suggestions that could be useful for doing this kind of analysis.

CONFIDENTIALITY

The necessity for confidentiality in counseling is well established. Clients need to be assured that what transpires in sessions will remain private. Without this confidence, they are not likely to reveal their concerns and divulge their hidden feelings and desires. Yet very few authorities suggest that confidentiality should be unlimited. If a client is in serious danger or a danger to others, or if a student reveals that he or she is being abused or contemplating suicide, most counselors probably would not hesitate to intervene. It seems reasonable to put the obligation to protect human lives above the obligation to maintain silence. For this reason, in most states counselors are required by law to report child abuse and to warn the potential victims of their clients.

However, the decision to maintain or break confidentiality can sometimes be very difficult. If a client comes to a session with multiple bruises or cigarette burns, or discloses that a rival gang member is going to get "wasted," the counselor's decision might be relatively simple. But the justification for violating anonymity is not always so obvious. The cases discussed in previous chapters provide examples of more difficult choices. When Jason revealed his father's educational program for him, Mr. Thompson wondered if more good or harm would result if he broke confidentiality and called a child protection agency. Ms. Larkin considered calling Maria's parents in spite of Maria's request that they not be told she was pregnant. Such situations occur where there are good reasons on both sides for different courses of action. A client is likely to see a broken confidence as a flagrant violation of trust. It may do irreparable harm to the counseling relationship. However, not doing so can sometimes involve serious risk to the client or others. A counselor may have to decide which course of action is likely to do the least harm.

One way to avert some ethical problems in this area is to discuss the limits of confidentiality before or during the first session with a client. What kinds of information cannot be kept private and why? To whom will the counselor disclose information? If the answers to these questions are provided at the outset, serious ethical problems regarding confidentiality may still occur, but at least the client will be aware of the limits to privacy, and should the counselor have to reveal information later, there is less likelihood that the counseling relationship will be destroyed.

CATEGORIZING AND LABELING

School counselors are routinely involved in the categorization and labeling of students. Large bureaucratized institutions like school districts cannot avoid grouping their clientele for various purposes. In some circumstances, grouping and labeling are relatively harmless. Students are "boys" or "girls," "sophomores" or "seniors," "locals" or "bused." However, some categorizations can have important long-range effects on students. When students are given labels like "mentally retarded," "emotionally disturbed," "hyperactive," or "incorrigible," the chances are that their academic programs and school-related social lives will be affected. They are likely to be treated differently from other students by faculty and their fellow students, and their chances of acquiring some of the benefits of the school program that are available to others may be reduced.

It does not follow that all labeling is unnecessary or evil. Identifying students with special needs and providing an appropriate program may enable them to benefit more from their school years. However, educators generally, and not just school counselors, should categorize and apply labels very cautiously with cognizance of both the short- and long-range consequences of what they are doing.

It is especially important for school counselors to recognize that they are inevitably involved in a categorization process as they work with students. From the moment a student enters the counseling office, questions run through the counselor's mind: What is the problem? Is it primarily the student's dilemma, or is it more complex? Is it a family problem, or one rooted in race or ethnicity? Is the conduct of the student at fault, or could the problem have originated in the eccentricities of a staff member? Does the situation involve one of the normal, growing up issues of youth, or is it sufficiently serious to warrant immediate, expert attention? Is this student dangerous to himself or herself or to others? As the counselor forms answers to questions like these, both the problem and the student are categorized. The difficulty is seen as "minor" or "severe," "psychological" or "social." The student is seen as "docile" or "hyperactive," "aggressor" or "innocent victim." These classifications shape the counselor's response to the situation.

Szasz (1974) and others have noted how various classifications and labels applied to persons influence the way others respond to them. Some designations like "incorrigible" or "delinquent" suggest that the situation is irremediable or calls for some form of punishment. Labels like "hyperactive" or "dyslexic" suggest physiological impairment that interferes with classroom functioning and requires corrective measures. "Mentally retarded" or "low IQ" suggest a limited potential for intellectual development. "Manic depressive" or "emotionally disturbed" indicate serious psychological problems. Labels like "exuberant," "loner," or "short-tempered" refer to behavior that is a little unusual but in the normal range. "Gifted" suggests that a person may be capable of great things.

The categorization of students is likely to have considerable influence on the way teachers and other students respond to them. They may be seen as (a) average students; (b) budding criminals, just a step or two from the penitentiary; (c) persons with little potential, not worth wasting much effort on; (d) persons whose inferior work or antisocial behavior is entirely attributable to physiological or psychological problems—and so, it would be useless to push them to do better; or (e) unusually capable students whose work is likely to be outstanding.

Counselors should maintain a healthy skepticism about the labels already attached to the students who come to them for help, as well as some caution regarding their own contributions to the way students are categorized. Labels not only affect the way others see and respond to us—they also affect the way we see ourselves. If classification is necessary, it must be done accurately and an effort made to ensure that the benefits to the student outweigh the possible harm.

INFLUENCING CLIENTS

Generally, the role of school counselors is to assist clients in making important decisions, not to tell them what to do. They provide students and their parents with information about the options in school and the requirements for entering various colleges. However, they hesitate to tell them which choices would be best for them. They are reluctant to tell parents how they should be raising their children or to tell students how to deal with personal problems. However, counselors willingly provide information about the agencies available to help clients with their uncertainties.

Although some counselors may not have formulated a clear rationale for their reluctance to advise, it probably stems from a commitment to the freedom principle—a belief that, *prima facie*, people ought to make their own decisions. They should not be forced, coerced, or manipulated by others. This leads to the conviction that school counselors should do everything they can to help students and parents to arrive at good choices, but should avoid making the choices for them. The ideal pattern for a counseling session might look like this:

1. A student or parent arrives with a problem.
2. The counselor helps the client to define the problem clearly, assess its seriousness, note all of the reasonable options, and identify the likely consequences and desirability of each.
3. The counselor gives support and encouragement to the client, as together they implement a plan to deal with the situation.

If counselors could stick to this scenario in working with students and parents, they would have few ethical problems related to the use of influence. Unfortunately, counselors cannot always maintain this role and on occasion must consider using more intrusive styles. Because of immaturity or emotional stress, clients may be unable to see their problems clearly, or they may be incapable of making a rational assessment of options. They may be committed to a line of action that looks clearly unreasonable and destructive to the counselor. What should counselors do when they have tried everything in their power to help a client form a positive plan to deal with a problem and, instead, the one the client creates will clearly result in harm to someone? Determining the appropriate response is not difficult if the likely damage is either extremely serious or only minor. For example, if a client reveals a plan for suicide or murder, the counselor should not hesitate to take virtually any measures necessary to prevent the action. Concern about interfering with the client's freedom of choice would be less important than preventing a death. If the harm in the client's plan is small, the counselor might decide that no intervention is warranted and that learning from experience might be good for the client. However, if the harm falls between these extremes, a more difficult decision regarding intrusive intervention may be needed. The following are possible choices for counselors, arranged roughly from a "quite mild" to a "quite strong" degree of intervention.

Intervention Alternatives for Influencing Client's Planned Action

1. In providing relevant information to the client, counselors could exaggerate the truth a little in order to make a dramatic presentation of the possible problems in the plan or display skepticism to any suggestions that make the proposal look attractive.
2. Counselors could disclose their own feelings about the proposition and tell the client what they see as the difficulties with the plan.
3. They could give direct advice to the client, such as, "I think it would be best to tell your parents right away that you are pregnant."
4. They could use subtle manipulations such as ignoring the client, giving looks of disapproval or disappointment when the person talks about implementing a plan that seems ill-advised, and using flattery for "unusual insight" when the client seems hesitant about going through with the plan.
5. Counselors could coerce a student by insisting that unless the plan is abandoned, the counseling relationship will have to be terminated or the plan disclosed to parents, school authorities, or police.

It is probably possible to think of sets of circumstances in which each of these strategies would be reasonable. Nevertheless, using any one may raise ethical questions connected with the lack of respect it manifests for the right of a client to deliberate freely. In the ideal situation, clients are entitled to think for themselves, make their own decisions about the best course of action, and follow through with the plan. It is ethical for others to help, but not for them to interfere.

Under some circumstances, any of the listed strategies could constitute undue interference. Skewing the truth can impede a client's deliberations. Under other conditions, disclosing one's own view or giving advice may increase the clients' dependence on the counselor and decrease their confidence to think through the problem for themselves. Manipulation and coercion put pressure on clients to take particular courses rather than coming to their own decision.

Of course, the foregoing does not mean that such common forms of influencing as modeling, advising, and self-disclosure are always invasions of a client's freedom and, hence, unethical.

For example, if a counselor advises a parent to join a group or attend some parenting classes, the advice has the potential to increase the person's range of possible responses to the child and to see more clearly what the implications of various responses are. If the advice leads to these results, the parent's freedom has been increased, not decreased. Even a threat to terminate a counseling relationship may result in an increase of freedom for a client under some conditions. If it succeeds in influencing a student to abandon a plan to become a drug dealer or to participate in a gang rumble, the long-range result is likely to be an increase in freedom. Furthermore, counselors may have a responsibility to help educate—and this includes morally educate—their clients. This would include trying to broaden their horizons, not just accepting them as given or fixed. Feminist counseling abounds with examples of this educational function at work.

School counselors are likely to have a significant influence on the lives of the students and the parents with whom they work. They should be aware of both the content and the form of influence they are using. The latter should reflect a concern both for preventing harm to the student and others and for encouraging independent judgment and responsibility in the client. The counselor's aim should be to provide help as unobtrusively as possible and to use stronger methods of influence only to prevent harm. (For a more complete discussion of this topic, see Schulte (1990).)

INSTITUTIONAL PRESSURES

Many potential ethical problems in school counseling stem from the setting in which they occur. Perhaps the best way to see how the school environment can generate ethical problems is to contrast the role of a school counselor with that of a counselor in private practice working with adults.

Counselors in private practice are likely to have considerable professional autonomy. They can usually decide to specialize in a specific methodology or restrict their practice to dealing with a limited range of problems. They can negotiate with clients about the problems to be addressed, the type of treatment to be used, the length and number of sessions needed, and so on. It is unlikely that others will try to make these decisions for them or raise objections to contracts made between counselors and clients.

School counseling is different in several important ways. Because schools are generally part of a large bureaucracy, school counselors are likely to have less professional autonomy. They are expected to comply with school board policies and school directives. The counseling program is likely to be organized in a hierarchy so that counselors' work must conform to policies established by the counseling arm of the school system. Ethical problems can occur as counselors find themselves pinned between an individual student or family and "the system." The policies that they are expected to follow may be quite reasonable when applied to large populations, but the problem of a specific student or family may fall "through the cracks." The counselors might have to decide whether violating or varying the interpretation of a policy to provide the help a student or family needs is justified—for example, tampering with personal data or test scores to enable a student to qualify for a special program.

The clients of school counselors are usually children; parents are likely to be interested in the reasons why someone at the school thinks their child needs counseling, what will occur in the sessions, what progress is made, and how the results of the counseling will affect their child's educational future. We have seen examples of how ethical problems can occur when a counselor must consider obligations to parents as well as the student. Ms. Larkin had difficulty deciding whether or not to involve Maria's family in decisions about her pregnancy. Mr. Thompson's case presents, perhaps, the most difficult kind of ethical problem involving parents. Counselors generally think of parents as a source of *help* for a student with a problem. What does a school counselor do when the parents are the *cause* of the student's problem?

Teachers are likely to have a vested interest in which students the school counselor sees, what kinds of problems are treated, and what happens to students as a result. It is not surprising that the chief concerns of classroom teachers are often their ability to run a successful educational program and to maintain order in the classroom. Most teachers are not indifferent to the problems of an individual student, but they may be compelled by institutional expectations and the press of time to give more attention to the progress of the class as a whole. A teacher who sees a student as a serious detriment to the class may look to the counselor as an agent who can assist in removing that student from the classroom, thus improving the learning conditions for others. Teachers may put pressure on counselors to recommend actions that might make a classroom run more smoothly but would be harmful to the individual student with whom the counselor is working. A school counselor might come between a teacher and a student, each with legitimate interests at stake. Whatever the counselor recommends may be seen as a betrayal by one or the other.

Although schools have many functions, their primary purpose is to provide an educational program. This means that counselors cannot restrict their concerns exclusively to the psychological and social needs of clients. The educational implications of counseling recommendations must also be considered. Fortunately, a student's educational problems often stem from a psychological or social problem, and alleviating these underlying causes enhances the student's chances of benefiting educationally. However, it is possible for personal needs to be in conflict with educational needs. For example, suppose a school counselor is working with a high-ability student who has a severe case of "math anxiety." Should the counselor accept the client's decision to avoid math classes or to take only elementary ones if doing so would jeopardize the student's academic future? Would it be better for counselors to encourage students to take the more demanding courses anyway and then help them find ways to handle the stress?

The educational needs of other students, besides the student the counselor is seeing, also must be given consideration. For example, it would not be justified for a school counselor to recommend that a classroom teacher devote more time to the personal problems of one student and ignore obligations to others. In most schools, institutional pressures are unavoidable, but school counselors can do some things to minimize them. As suggested earlier, counselors can have a clear understanding with administrators, teachers, students, and parents regarding the guidelines for counseling—that is, what problems and procedures are appropriate for counseling sessions, and what will be reported and what will be kept confidential.

Another way to reduce the ethical damage of institutional pressures is to avoid apathy or resignation in response to directives that filter down through the bureaucracy. If it looks as if a new policy will interfere with providing adequate counseling, the counselors can make their concerns known and, if necessary, initiate appropriate action to have the policy modified or withdrawn.

It is also important for school counselors to avoid counseling myopia. They should do their best to see the school from the perspective of the other professionals who work there. Administrators and teachers have legitimate concerns that cannot be ignored. The more fully counselors understand the institution as a complex social system, the better they will be able to find ways to help clients.

SUMMARY

Perhaps a school counselor's most serious ethical problem is to think that there are no such problems or that they can be solved with little or no effort. This superficial thinking can lead to conclusions such as the following:

- There is an appropriate counseling response for any situation, and I was thoroughly trained before I came to the job. I don't need a lot of ethical analysis to decide what to do.
- As long as I stay within the law and school board policies, I know I won't get into trouble. Who needs ethics?
- I don't have to do any thinking about ethics. In my heart of hearts, I can feel whether something is right or wrong.

By now, there should be no need to point out the problems with these positions. Ethical problems in school counseling are both inevitable and serious, and giving them careful analysis and responding to them are among the important responsibilities of counselors.

CHAPTER 7

A Sample Analysis: The Case of Jennifer

Jennifer, a 16-year-old student, tells her school counselor that she is fed up with both her home life and the school program. She is going to join her 19-year-old boyfriend in another city. She says that he has a fairly steady job and thinks he makes enough money to support both of them until she finds work. She has no intention of telling her parents about her plans because she knows that her mother would try to stop her.

* * *

The following is a list of the tasks essential for any case analysis:

1. Identify alternative responses to the situation and their likely consequences.
2. Determine what information is crucial to selecting an ethical response and obtain that information:
   - facts about the client's situation and problems;
   - relevant school policies;
   - relevant laws and court decisions; and
   - relevant guidelines from professional codes of ethics.
3. Apply the four fundamental principles to the case.
4. Develop case-specific ethical principles.
5. Identify the ethical issues presented by the case.
6. Build the best ethical arguments possible to support the more plausible responses to the situation.
7. Determine which course of action is most ethically justified.

ANALYZING THE CASE

The real test of a counselor's grasp of ethical reasoning and its applications is the way he or she responds to specific, difficult ethical problems.

Despite the fact that most of these problems have common elements and that some tasks of analysis are essential in addressing any school counseling case, no one step-by-step procedure is best for conducting all case analyses. The following are some examples of alternative actions and their likely consequences for the school counselor confronted with Jennifer's case.

Alternative Responses in the Case of Jennifer

1. *Maintain routine counseling procedures.* Jennifer should explore her feelings about the situation and her reasons for wanting to run away. From that, it might be possible to determine whether she has thought through the consequences and recognizes the difficulties in her plan. The counselor could help her identify and evaluate a number of ways to deal with the problems she is facing and come to her own conclusion about the best course of action to take, without interfering or trying to influence her toward or away from any alternative response. The likely result of this approach is that Jennifer would leave school and join her boyfriend. The prognosis for teenagers who take this alternative is not favorable. The chances are that the relationship would not last, and Jennifer would be in an unfamiliar environment with many problems and very little support. Meanwhile, her mother would be frightened and worried about Jennifer's safety. If she found out that school personnel had known of the plan beforehand, she would be angered and might consider legal action. However, there is always the possibility that Jennifer might decide to stay at home and work on some less hazardous way of dealing with her problems.
2. *Inform Jennifer's parents about her plan.* Jennifer should be encouraged to communicate with her mother herself or allow the counselor to talk with her. But, assuming that these options fail, Jennifer should be informed that the counselor is required to notify her parents because she is a minor, and her safety and welfare are at stake. Jennifer's parents could be contacted without disclosing her plan to run away. They could be invited in for a general discussion of Jennifer's problems. The chances are that they would not come, and if they did, setting up a meeting would take time. It would probably be too late to do anything to prevent Jennifer from leaving. If the counselor did reveal Jennifer's plan to her parents, it might prevent her from taking a dangerous step, but it is also likely that she would feel abandoned and betrayed, and the possibility of a further working relationship with her would be very slim.

3. *Report Jennifer's plan to the school administrators.* No doubt, they would take some immediate action to stop Jennifer from running away. They would inform her parents, as well as take other measures to stop her. The results would probably be the same as informing her parents: Jennifer's plan to run away would be squelched, but her hostility to school, in general, and to the counselor, in particular, would increase. Their relationship would probably be at an end.

DETERMINING AND OBTAINING CRITICAL INFORMATION

School counselors often lack vital information when attempting to find the best way to deal with a complex case. They frequently carry heavy workloads, which makes it difficult for them to do the time-consuming research for any particular case. Although they are likely to have a general understanding of their legal obligations to students, parents, and the school district, they do not have the time or expertise to investigate the fine points of law that may be relevant. They are also likely to have a general understanding of the kinds of families living in their community, their problems and concerns, but not to have much firsthand knowledge of the family backgrounds of the students who are currently their clients. The information that they do have is likely to come from the students and parents themselves in private sessions and, in many cases, may be biased and self-serving. What sorts of information should Jennifer's counselor seek and which are likely to be found?

Crucial Information in the Case of Jennifer

1. *Client's age.* The counselor would want this information because legal obligations regarding both students and their parents may vary according to the age of the student. Jennifer is 16.
2. *Client's school record.* The counselor would want some background in order to understand the client's school concerns and to help assess the likelihood of her benefiting from the school program if she were to remain. Jennifer's school records indicate low-average work. She has been absent often, but not enough to suggest truancy. She has not participated in any extracurricular activities. Her academic progress has been satisfactory, and she has no serious conduct violations on her record. Nothing in her file indicates that she would be unable to complete her high school education.

3. *Client's personal life.* The counselor would want to know as much as possible about Jennifer's life outside school. This information is important for assessing the client's own interpretation of the situation and her plans to cope with it. Jennifer says that her father is a virtual stranger to her. He works long hours, and when he comes home, he only wants to lie on the sofa in front of the TV with a six-pack of beer. Her younger brother is also seldom at home. He hangs out with a gang, but so far has not been in any serious trouble. She says it is her mother who is ruining her life with ceaseless nagging about her unwillingness to share the housekeeping chores, her untidy appearance, her unacceptable school work, and her deadbeat friends. She tells Jennifer constantly that her boyfriend is worthless and has forbidden her to spend time with him. He was kicked out of high school about two years ago for selling small quantities of marijuana. Jennifer says he does not sell or use drugs anymore. Jennifer has no close friends at school and has not developed an important relationship with any of her teachers. None of her classes seem worthwhile to her.
4. *Relevant school policies.* When counselors take a position in a school, they agree, at least tacitly, that they will act in accordance with its policies. If they discover a policy or directive that seems unethical or unreasonable for some reason, it would be wise to make their concerns known to the authorities immediately and attempt to remedy the problem with the policy before harm is done to clients or others. Fortunately, no school policies in effect at Jennifer's high school would constitute barriers in the counselor's attempt to help her deal with the problems she is experiencing.
5. *Relevant laws and court decisions.* Counselors are not lawyers but can be expected to have a good grasp of the legal obligations to students, parents, the school district, and other agencies and institutions connected with their work. They should also know where to seek answers to legal questions that arise. The legal obligations of a counselor working on a case like Jennifer's could be quite difficult to determine. Perhaps the most pressing question is whether the counselor is legally obliged to inform Jennifer's parents about her plans to run away. Gustafson and McNamara (1987) point out that state laws vary concerning the relationship between counselors and minor clients. Some protect the confidence of minors in counseling and others require that important information acquired from them to be shared with their parents. Let us assume that the counselor in this case investigates the legal obligations and finds that they cannot be clearly established. Court cases in the state suggest that, since

Jennifer is over 12 years old, the counselor probably has no legal obligation to breach confidentiality unless Jennifer or others are in imminent danger of serious harm.

6. *Relevant guidelines from professional codes of ethics.* Although school counselors are ultimately responsible for the judgments they make and the actions they take, the burden of determining what is ethical and unethical in school counseling is not theirs alone. Professional organizations have grappled with important ethical questions in the field and have provided guidelines to identify and clarify the ethical responsibilities of their members. The school counselor in this case would be wise to look for relevant guidelines in the two documents in Appendixes A and B: Ethical Standards of the American Counseling Association (ACA) and Ethical Standards for School Counselors of the American School Counselor Association (ASCA).

INTERPRETING THE PROFESSIONAL CODES OF ETHICS

In the following lists of considerations relevant to our case, the letter and number designations of the items in the original documents are included in parentheses. (See Appendixes A and B for the complete professional codes of ethics of the ACA and ASCA.)

ACA Standards Relevant to Jennifer's Case

1. The counselor has responsibilities to both the individual who is the client and to the institution within which the counseling services are offered. (A.2)
2. The counselor recognizes his or her boundaries of competence. (A.7)
3. The counselor recognizes the client's need for freedom of choice, and apprises the client of necessary restrictions that may limit freedom of choice. (B.Preamble)
4. The counselor's primary obligation is to respect the integrity and promote the welfare of the client.
5. The counselor keeps information acquired in the counseling relationship confidential. (B.2)
6. If the client's condition indicates that there is clear and imminent danger to the parties involved, the counselor takes reasonable personal action or informs authorities. In this situation, the counselor consults with other professionals if possible. The counselor assumes responsibility for the client's behavior only after careful deliberation and returns responsibility to the client as soon as possible. (B.4)

7. At or before the time that counseling is entered, when working with a minor or a person who is unable to give consent, the counselor protects the client's best interest. The counselor informs the client of the purposes, goals, techniques, rules of procedure, and limitations that may affect the relationship. (B.8)
8. The counselor may choose to consult with other professionally competent persons about the client, but should avoid placing a consultant in a conflict of interest situation. (B.11)
9. If the counselor determines that he or she is unable to be of professional assistance to the client, a counseling relationship should be avoided or immediately terminated and appropriate alternatives found. (B.12)

Many of the same considerations are suggested in "Ethical Standards for School Counselors." However, this document proposes some further ethical obligations, and some of the obligations suggested above are given more specificity.

ASCA Standards Relevant to Jennifer's Case

1. The counselor has a primary obligation and loyalty to the pupils and treats the pupils with respect as unique individuals. (A.1)
2. The counselor is concerned with the total needs of the pupils and encourages maximum growth and development of clients. (A.2)
3. The counselor respects the inherent rights and responsibilities of parents for their children and endeavors to establish a cooperative relationship with parents to facilitate the maximum development of clients. (B.1)
4. The counselor provides parents with accurate, comprehensive, and relevant information in an objective and caring manner. (B.3)
5. The counselor establishes and maintains a cooperative relationship with faculty, staff, and administration to facilitate the provision of optimal guidance and counseling services. (C.1)
6. The counselor adheres to ethical standards of the profession, other official policy statements pertaining to counseling, and relevant statutes established by federal, state, and local governments. (F.4)

Note that these guidelines would be helpful to the school counselor working on Jennifer's case by identifying some important points to consider. However, the codes of ethics by themselves are not likely to solve the counselor's problem. Here are some examples of the specific difficulties of applying the ethical standards of the codes.

Questions in Applying the Standards to Jennifer's Case

1. *Is the counselor ethically obliged to involve school administrators in this case or ethically obliged to exclude them?* The codes suggest that the school counselor has responsibilities both to clients and to the institution; but in our complex case, it is not clear how one balances these commitments. If Jennifer does run away, her action may have serious consequences for the school administration, such as a lawsuit. Yet, the counselor is also obliged by the codes to respect the client's freedom of choice and to keep confidential what transpires in counseling sessions. The codes do not indicate under what conditions counselors should consult with administrators.
2. *Is the counselor in this case obliged to involve Jennifer's parents in the case or to honor Jennifer's request to exclude them?* The codes oblige a school counselor to respect the rights and responsibilities of parents regarding their children, which includes sharing important information with them, but it also obliges the counselor to respect the integrity and freedom of choice of the client.
3. *Is the counselor required only to help Jennifer come to her own decision, or are a variety of other interventions justified by the codes?* The codes say that the counselor should maintain "loyalty to the client," "promote the client's welfare," and "encourage maximum growth and development." How should these phrases be interpreted in this case?

APPLYING THE FUNDAMENTAL ETHICAL PRINCIPLES

Let us now consider how the four fundamental principles—considering interests, maximizing freedom, respecting truth, and valuing equality—could be interpreted in this case.

Considering Interests

A school counselor is likely to experience two kinds of ethical problems that are related to this principle. The first is determining how to respond to the legitimate and, perhaps, conflicting interests of several persons in a situation. It seems apparent that Jennifer's interests should be the primary concern of the counselor. However, Jennifer is not the only one who will be significantly affected by the counselor's response. Serious consideration must be given to the interests of Jennifer's parents, as well as to the position of the school administration.

The second problem related to the application of this principle occurs when a counselor's assessment of what is in a client's best interests conflicts with the client's assessment. The counselor is well aware that, in general at least, teenage girls who leave their families to live with boyfriends in different cities do not fare well. On the basis of discussions with Jennifer, the counselor must decide whether Jennifer's interests are better served by helping her to plan the move or by taking some action to stop her. Her thoughts might run something like this:

> *Perhaps it is presumptuous of me to assume that my judgment about what is in Jennifer's interest is better than her own.* Jennifer is fairly mature for a girl of 16. From what she says, it appears that she has no strong ties to her family or school and is not receiving much support from either. She has made up her mind that she will have a much better chance for happiness by leaving her family and school and joining her boyfriend. It may be in Jennifer's interest to face the problems connected with starting a new life in a different environment. She has shown a reasonable grasp of the risks connected with what she intends to do. She has formed a plan and is intent on following it.
>
> *However, in spite of our discussions, I am not sure that she is mature enough to evaluate her own plan realistically. My inclination is to do what I can to dissuade her from leaving.* Her judgment seems a bit clouded both by her strong attraction to her boyfriend and her desire to escape the constant criticisms of her mother. What she intends to do is very risky. At present, she has some security, a place to live, regular meals, and people who care about her welfare.
>
> *Perhaps I should talk to the parents in this case. If Jennifer were my daughter, I would be very resentful if others deprived me of the opportunity to be involved in her problems and plans to deal with them.* I have had no personal contact with Jennifer's parents. I know little about them beyond what Jennifer has told me. However, the upbringing of a child is primarily the responsibility of the parents, and they should play a major role in important decisions. It seems that it is in the interest of Jennifer's parents to know that their daughter is planning such a radical move.
>
> *It is in the administration's interest to have information that is important for maintaining the quality of the school program and good school-community relations. Perhaps I have an obligation to involve Ms. Johnson in the case in some way.* I have had a good relationship with Ms. Johnson, the school principal. She understands that it is very important for me to keep my promise to clients that what occurs in counseling sessions will be confidential. When I was assigned to this school, she said she only wanted information that was important for per-

forming her duties as the chief administrator of the school. That seems like a reasonable request. If Jennifer leaves and it becomes public knowledge that school personnel knew of her plans, Jennifer's mother would probably be very irate and might initiate a lawsuit. School-community relations could be seriously strained.

Maximizing Freedom

Maximizing the freedom of another person can involve either negative or positive action or both, depending on the person and the circumstances. The negative interpretation of the principle is to refrain from imposing restrictions on the choices and actions of others or on their deliberations about what actions to take. The positive interpretation is to assist a person actively in determining what action is desirable and overcoming barriers that restrict the person's deliberations or actions. The counselor who is working with Jennifer has an ethical problem regarding the appropriate application of this principle:

> *If I try to stop Jennifer from going, by some strong intervention like telling her parents or reporting her plan to the principal, it seems like I am interfering with her freedom rather than maximizing it.* Jennifer and I have talked at some length about her plan to join her boyfriend. She seems to know what she is getting into. In our talks, I have helped her compare the likely consequences of staying and leaving and to identify the advantages and disadvantages of each choice. If I take a stronger role in her decision by telling her that I think she is making a big mistake or by pleading with her to reconsider, it also seems like I would be interfering. I would be trying to skew her thinking more favorably toward my choice of action and away from hers.
>
> *Perhaps taking actions to deter her or at least to delay her from leaving would be a way of maximizing her freedom.* On the other hand, I am not sure that Jennifer is capable of thinking objectively about her choices now. She is only 16 and has a strong urge to leave home to be with her boyfriend. Perhaps she is not free enough of her own emotions and shortsightedness to make the best choice for herself. After all, it could easily happen that she ends up in strange surroundings, perhaps pregnant, and without much financial or any other kind of support. If freedom means being able to make choices, act on them, and reap the benefits one expects from those actions, the chances are that Jennifer's move will bring her even less freedom than she has now. She is likely to have even less control over her

own life. Perhaps, if I intervened in some way to deter her, I could help her to achieve the maturity and stability she needs to face problems realistically and make good choices to deal with them. She would probably see my intervention as paternalistic and as an unjustified restriction of her freedom, but perhaps, in the long run, it would be a way of increasing her freedom.

Respecting Truth

Respect for truth entails both negative and positive obligations. Intentionally deceiving others is probably the most obvious violation of the principle. However, when the principle is applied to the counseling relationship, it would seem to obligate the counselor to do more than just refrain from deception. When a counselor accepts a person as a client, a commitment is made to work with that person to overcome the problems identified as the focus for the counseling sessions. Helping clients to deal with their problems entails, among other things, helping them to see their situation as fully and accurately as possible, to avoid self-deception, and to acquire any information that might enable them to deal more effectively with the situation. It also involves helping them to make an accurate appraisal of alternative responses. In all of these ways of assisting clients, counselors are obligated to show an unwavering concern for truth. Unfortunately, it is not always easy for a counselor to ascertain the truth. When the counselor's information about a client's problem and background comes primarily from the client, it is not easy to assess the accuracy of what one has learned. This problem is illustrated in the case of Jennifer. Regarding the application of the respect for truth principle, the counselor might have to question the accuracy of some of the information that has been presented:

> *I have no reason to suspect that Jennifer is lying to me, but I have to admit that I really am not certain what the situation is.* Jennifer says that the situation at home is intolerable, and that the demands of her mother are impossible. She says that things will be much better for her in another city when she is living with her boyfriend. She says that he has a good job and is no longer peddling drugs. We have discussed these things at some length. However, I cannot ignore the fact that she is only 16 and may not be seeing her home situation and the prospects of life with her boyfriend very accurately. I have had several adolescent clients in the past who sincerely believed that their problems with their parents were insurmountable and that

the only solution was running away. But often the alleged crises turned out to be only minor squabbles about appropriate attire for dates or curfew deadlines. Now I have to decide whether or not to take some action to stop, or at least delay, Jennifer from leaving. My decision must be based on my judgment of the seriousness of her situation.

Maybe I should have been more clear about the limits of my promise of confidentiality. I could probably get a better picture if I were able to talk with Jennifer's parents, but Jennifer will not agree to this. At the beginning of our counseling relationship, I promised Jennifer that everything that happened in our sessions would be kept confidential unless I believed that she or someone else were in serious and imminent danger. I wonder if Jennifer's situation is serious enough to justify breaking confidentiality and calling her parents. If I did this, there is little doubt that Jennifer would feel betrayed. She would think that I lied to her when I promised to keep our sessions private. Goodness knows, I had no intention of deceiving her when I made the promise.

Valuing Equality

The equality principle obligates a counselor to give equal concern to all clients. It also obligates the counselor to give consideration to the relevant differences among clients when responding to them. It does not appear that concern for equality is the central issue in this case. However, the counselor is having some difficulty deciding whether to help Jennifer make up her own mind about what she wants to do or to intervene actively to deter her from leaving. The equality principle is relevant to this consideration.

The hypothetical counselor who is working with Jennifer is committed to allowing as much freedom to clients as possible to settle their own problems and promises clients confidentiality unless there are indications of serious consequences. The equality principle obligates the counselor to justify treating Jennifer in a different manner from other clients. Taking some action to deter Jennifer from following her own plans for dealing with her problems, or breaking confidentiality regarding her plans, would be a departure from the norm and could only be justified by reference to the specific circumstances of the case. For example, the counselor might come to the conclusion that the danger to Jennifer is severe enough to override concern for client self-direction and respect for confidentiality.

DEVELOPING CASE-SPECIFIC ETHICAL PRINCIPLES

Many quite specific ethical principles are suggested both by a review of Jennifer's case itself and the discussion to this point. As we pointed out in Chapter 4, there are three important requirements for developing sound, case-specific, ethical principles: They must be directly relevant to the case; they must be ethical imperatives rather than mere rules of prudence or politeness; and they must be capable of being ethically justified by connecting them with well-established, higher-level principles.

Specific Principles in Jennifer's Case

1. School counselors should foster autonomy in clients and encourage them to take the initiative in identifying problems and making plans to deal with them.
2. They should work as closely as possible with parents to help their children.
3. They should do everything that can reasonably be done to protect a client from harm.
4. They should work closely with school faculty and administrators to maintain and improve the academic program and school-community relations.
5. School counselors should keep what transpires in counseling sessions confidential. They should consider breaking confidentiality only when the client or others are in clear and imminent danger.

IDENTIFYING THE ETHICAL ISSUES

In order to identify the ethical issues in this or any other case, one needs an understanding of what makes a problem an *ethical* issue. Humans have many kinds of problems, in areas such as health, economics, and family relationships. What distinguishes an ethical issue from other kinds of problems is that it involves ethical principles. Ethical principles, in effect, create ethical problems. This is why the discussion in Chapters 4 and 5 is so essential; it "creates" the ethical perspective and all that follows from it.

Where the ethical domain enters into the counseling experience, the counselor's obligation may be the moral education of the client. That is, if the client's presenting problem is psychological (such as undue anxiety or depression), the underlying causes might be ethical. Helping clients entails assisting them to understand the ethical dimensions of their situations.

The Ethical Issues in Jennifer's Case

1. The counselor is ethically obligated to give Jennifer as much freedom as possible to make her own decisions, but the counselor is also obligated to take reasonable action to prevent harm from coming to Jennifer. *Should the counselor intervene to prevent or deter Jennifer from running away? If so, just what sort of intervention is ethically justified?*
2. The counselor is ethically obligated to recognize that parents have the primary responsibility for raising children and to help them in any reasonable way. So, on learning that a student is in a dangerous situation, the counselor is obligated to inform the child's parents. But the counselor is also obligated to keep a promise that the counseling sessions will be kept confidential unless there is serious, imminent danger. *Is the counselor obligated to contact Jennifer's parents, or to maintain confidentiality? Is there any action in regard to Jennifer's parents that the counselor is obligated to take?*
3. The counselor is obligated to work cooperatively with the faculty and administrators and abide by an agreement with the principal to keep him or her informed of any situation that is important for maintaining the quality of the academic program and good school-community relations. However, the counselor is also obligated to maintain confidentiality. *Is the counselor obligated to contact the principal regarding Jennifer's situation?*

BUILDING ETHICAL ARGUMENTS

With the various tasks of analysis now completed, what sort of ethical arguments could be applied to support various courses of action? Several strategies are available to address this task. For example, the counselor could focus on one issue at a time and ethical arguments and counterarguments regarding various responses to that issue could be developed. This might be the most thorough approach, but it would likely take too long. Perhaps the business could be accomplished adequately, more quickly, and more dramatically by imagining two different school counselors who are in disagreement over how to respond to the case. They will each identify what they see as the best decision for Jennifer's counselor to take, and present arguments to show why that particular course of action is, to their way of thinking, the most ethically justified.

Plan A: Maintaining Confidentiality

Counselor A believes that Jennifer's counselor should not make any dramatic departure from normal school counseling procedures. At the outset, the counselor promised Jennifer that what would transpire in their counseling sessions would be kept confidential unless Jennifer said something to indicate serious and imminent danger to herself or others. If the counselor takes some precipitous action now, like informing Jennifer's parents or the school principal that Jennifer is planning to leave, she would be breaking a sacred promise and destroying Jennifer's trust. Such action would be an unjustified invasion of Jennifer's freedom to be in charge of her own life. It is true that she is only 16, but she has shown enough maturity to grasp the significance of her decision to leave. Jennifer recognizes that she will face many hazards in her new life and will bring much distress to her mother by leaving. However, it would be wrong for the counselor to consider either of these consequences as sufficient grounds for taking steps to stop her from going. Nothing suggests that the danger to her is serious enough to justify depriving her of the right to deliberate and choose her own course of action.

A school counselor is ethically obliged to work cooperatively with parents and administrators, but this does not necessarily mean informing either of them when a student is contemplating some risky behavior. If counselors did contact parents or administrators every time students discussed potentially dangerous actions that they had taken or were considering, no students would come to the counseling office voluntarily, or, if they did, they would never reveal the things that were really troubling them. Perhaps, if Jennifer were only 12 years old, if she were leaving with no plan for taking care of her needs, or if she showed no recognition of the risks involved, the counselor's obligation to protect her from danger would override the promises to maintain confidentiality and protect her freedom. None of these conditions exist here. Administrators and parents have been informed that, unless there is serious and imminent danger, the counselor is not obliged to tell them anything.

Plan B: Informing Parents

Counselor B maintains that Jennifer's counselor is ethically bound to contact the parents and warn them that their daughter is about to run away, even though this action will likely cause severe damage to the counselor's relationship with Jennifer. When parents give their permission for their children to see the school counselor, they assume that this person is there to help them provide for the development of their children, to understand problems that they may be experiencing, and to keep open the lines of communication between them. When a minor is planning a course of action as fraught with danger as Jennifer is now, the counselor cannot just let it happen. The parents must be informed so that they can take steps to protect their child. When counselors work with clients of any age, they should encourage them to take the initiative in identifying the issues and determining the best ways to deal with them. Counselors are ethically obliged to encourage freedom and responsibility in their clients. But Jennifer is not yet ready to manage her life without some guidance. Parents are usually the ones to provide the help that children like Jennifer need. Right now, Jennifer's relationship with her mother looks dismal but not hopeless, because it is clear that her mother cares what happens to her.

The counselor should do everything within reason to influence Jennifer to delay or abandon her plan to run away and to establish lines of communication with her mother. The counselor could suggest that the two of them come in together for counseling or recommend family counseling for all members. The counselor could disclose a personal concern about Jennifer's welfare and encourage her to reconsider her plan to run away. If these strategies fail, there is no ethically justified alternative except to tell Jennifer that, in the judgment of the counselor, she is in imminent danger, and her parents must be notified. It should be emphasized how sorry the counselor is to have to take this action and Jennifer should be encouraged to continue coming in for counseling sessions. Similarly, when informing the parents, the counselor should make a sincere effort to involve them in the counseling and encourage them to develop bonds of understanding and trust with their daughter. These steps are important because of the serious harm that may be done by breaking confidentiality and the ethical obligation to make every effort to continue to help Jennifer resolve her problems.

Although the counselor is ethically obligated to inform Jennifer's parents of her plan, there is no justification for telling anyone else. If a counselor is ethically compelled to violate confidentiality, the breach should be made as small as possible. The justification is protection of a student from danger. The best agency for protecting the student in a case like this is the parents. There is no reason to inform the principal. If a counselor learns that an important exam has been stolen from a file or that there is a plan to vandalize the school, then there would be ethical justification for informing the administrators. In such circumstances, the integrity of the academic program or the welfare of the whole school community is in jeopardy. These are the legitimate concerns of school administrators, and the counselor is ethically obligated to take reasonable action to help prevent the harm from occurring. However, in this case, the only one in danger is Jennifer, and her parents are in the best position to protect her.

The final task of analysis is left to the reader. Does Counselor A or Counselor B suggest the course of action that is more ethically justified? Who offers the more convincing ethical arguments? Perhaps a third course of action is better than that prescribed by either A or B. If so, what arguments can be developed to support it?

CHAPTER 8

Cases for Discussion

Although earlier chapters use cases to illustrate particular kinds of ethical problems, most cases pose a wide variety of issues to ponder. This chapter presents many more cases, as well as questions, to help identify the specific problems presented. It might be useful to review the suggestions for case analysis in Chapter 6 and also to refer to the ethical standards in Appendixes A and B to determine if any standards included there are relevant.

Case analysis is done most fruitfully in small groups. Different observations, even clashing views, can contribute to everyone's ethical thinking. There are no recipes for solving the ethical problems of counseling, nor is there one sequence of steps that is the best for analyzing every kind of ethical dilemma. However, the following are some general suggestions for analyses of the cases in this chapter:

1. Consider what is ethically at stake in the situation. What ethical principles might apply? Whose interests are at risk and how?
2. Sketch two or three plausible responses that the school counselor might make. For each response, consider the consequences that would likely follow, the ethical reasons supporting the response, and the ethical problems and risks entailed.
3. Determine which response is most ethically justified. Explain why that particular response would be the best one, or would likely do the least harm.
4. Consider to what extent the problems presented in the case were predictable and whether some action could have been taken to prevent them from occurring.

CASE ONE: STUDENT MAKES STRONG CLAIMS ABOUT AN INSTRUCTOR

During a counseling session, a boy says that he hates a particular male physical education instructor. He says the teacher has a violent temper, uses profanity constantly, and has made vague threats about physically harming the student. The counselor has heard that this individual is an intense sort of person but has never heard anything before to suggest that students working with him might be in danger. The student is unwilling to make a public complaint against the instructor or to meet with him in the presence of the counselor.

Questions to Consider

1. Since the student is unwilling to reveal to others his concerns about the instructor, is any action by the counselor justified?
2. Should the counselor conduct an independent investigation of the situation? What would be the justification?
3. Should the counselor tell the principal about the student's complaints? On what would this decision be based?
4. Should the instructor be given any notification regarding the student's complaint? What would be the reasons for such action?

CASE TWO: STUDENT WANTS ADVANCED CLASSES

The counselor is helping Kimberley, a high school junior, decide on her program for the coming year. Kimberley insists that she must be enrolled in advanced mathematics and science classes. The counselor notes that she had to repeat an earlier math class and has barely passed others in science and mathematics. When asked why she is so adamant about taking more classes in these subjects, Kimberley says that she loves the ocean and decided long ago that marine biology would be the ideal career for her.

Questions to Consider

1. Should the counselor discourage Kimberley from taking the classes she wants? What would be the grounds for this?
2. Should the counselor discourage Kimberley from pursuing a career in marine biology? On what basis could this be justified?

CASE THREE: WHITE COUNSELOR WANTS BLACK COLLEAGUE TO COUNSEL BLACK STUDENTS

The high school student body is roughly three-quarters white and one-quarter black. The counseling staff consists of one white and one black counselor. The training and experience of the two counselors is quite similar. One morning, the white counselor makes the following suggestion: "From now on, why don't you take all the black students and their families. You understand their problems better, and they probably feel more comfortable working with you."

Questions to Consider

1. Does the proposed policy seem reasonable? What problems or benefits would likely occur if the policy were implemented?
2. Would it be a better idea to allow students to ask for the counselor they wish to see? If so, should their requests always be honored? Under what circumstances should they be respected or denied?
3. What would be the best policy for deciding to whom a student be assigned? How would one determine this?

CASE FOUR: STUDENT WANTS TO KNOW COUNSELOR'S OWN VIEW

Darlene, a 10th-grade girl, is telling the counselor about arguments with her parents concerning her relationship with her boyfriend, an active gang member who has had many encounters with the law. As the student describes the relationship, the counselor realizes that her parents have plenty to worry about. In the middle of the discussion, the student becomes somewhat defensive. She says, "I can tell by your questions and the look on your face that you agree with my parents. You think I should break it off with Mike? Am I right?"

Questions to Consider

1. Do you think that the counselor should share personal views with Darlene about her relationship with her boyfriend and what she ought to do about it? Are there ethical reasons for telling or not telling her?
2. Do you think that the counselor should take any actions to discourage Darlene from continuing the relationship with her boyfriend? Which actions would be ethically justified and which would not?

CASE FIVE: STUDENT INVOLVED IN A CRIME

During a counseling session, Kevin, an 11th-grade student, reveals that he was involved in a car theft last weekend, although it was not his idea, and he was not the one who actually stole the car. During the first session with this student, the counselor reviewed the policy regarding confidentiality: Information about criminal activity was one of the exceptions. However, the counselor is still inclined toward maintaining silence. Kevin is not a hard-core gang member, and continuing to work with him may help him stay out of the criminal justice system.

Questions to Consider

1. Do you think that the counselor is ethically justified in departing from stated policy in this case? What would be the reasons for or against this decision?
2. Do you think that the counselor is obligated to report the crime, and if so, to whom? Is the counselor obligated to tell everything that Kevin has revealed? Should the counseling relationship with him continue?

CASE SIX: COUNSELOR WANTS TO GIVE STUDENT MORE COUNSELING TIME

Ms. Phillips is an overworked school counselor trying her best to provide her services to all who need her help. She has just finished a session with Susan, a 7th-grade student with a variety of academic and personal problems. She has excellent rapport with Susan and knows she could be a big help to her if only there were more time. She is considering inviting Susan to meet with her at her home on Saturdays.

Questions to Consider

1. If Ms. Phillips decides to meet with Susan on Saturdays, how might this action affect their counseling relationship? How might it affect her counseling relationship with other clients?
2. Are there any conditions under which Ms. Phillips would be ethically justified in meeting with Susan on Saturdays?

CASE SEVEN: FATHER WANTS STUDENT TO GO TO WORK FOR HIM

The client is Jorge, an Hispanic male and high school senior. He has maintained a remarkable academic record in the areas of science and mathematics. He has come to the counseling office because several faculty members have urged him to find out about scholarships and financial assistance programs available at local colleges. After the counselor gives him some of this information, he blurts out, "O.K. That's enough. Thank you for your time. I guess the whole idea is pretty silly. I'm not going to college. My father is counting on me to work with him in his yard-care business when school is over. He talks about it all the time. He couldn't take it if I told him I wasn't going to work for him. I just can't disappoint him."

Questions to Consider

1. Should the counselor take any action to influence Jorge to change his decision? What would be the grounds for this?
2. Should the counselor contact Jorge's father to try to convince him that his son should go to college?

CASE EIGHT: STUDENT'S FRIENDS MAY BE A BAD INFLUENCE ON HER

Diane, a very quiet and shy 9th-grader, has recently started hanging around with four girls, each of whom has been suspended from school several times. The offenses have included truancy, smoking on campus, and defiance of authority. Diane has no record of bad conduct and has earned average grades in previous semesters. However, several of her teachers have noted that her work is deteriorating, and they attribute the decline to her new group of friends. They hope some action can be taken before it is too late.

Questions to Consider

1. Is there any ethical justification for influencing Diane to end the relationship with her new girlfriends? What would be the ethical basis for this decision?
2. Is there anything that the counselor should do to help Diane?

CASE NINE: STUDENT INTENDS TO CHEAT

Allen is a senior and under great pressure to be an academic success. His parents tell him constantly that he must attain excellent grades so that he can enter a prestigious university and become a respected and high-paid professional, like his father. During a session with the school counselor, he reveals that he intends to use crib notes during a chemistry exam scheduled for that afternoon. He says that the instructor grades "on the curve," and many students in the class cheat on the tests. Therefore, he has to do it, too, so he can maintain his good scholastic record.

Questions to Consider

1. Should the counselor try to stop Allen from going ahead with his plan? What means should be used?
2. Should the counselor warn the instructor about Allen's intention to cheat?

CASE TEN: STUDENT THINKS THAT HER TRUANCY IS JUSTIFIED

Brenda admits to her school counselor that her many absences during the past month constitute truancy, but she expresses no remorse and says she has no intention of changing her ways. She claims that the school offers her nothing, and she backs up her claim with several examples of classes in which her own interests were completely ignored and the demands of the instructor totally unreasonable. From personal experience, the counselor believes that there is probably much truth in Brenda's complaints.

Questions to Consider

1. Would the counselor be justified in terminating the counseling relationship and threatening to refer the case to the school administrators for disciplinary action unless Brenda promises to stop skipping school?
2. Should the counselor investigate Brenda's complaints about her classes and, possibly, inform the principal about them?
3. If the counselor receives several reports about incompetent or unethical practices by teachers in their classrooms, is the counselor obligated to intervene? If so, then what action should be taken?

CASE ELEVEN: PARENT OPPOSES PLACEMENT OF STUDENT

The school psychologist, two classroom teachers, and the school counselor all agree that the best placement for Billy, a 4th-grade student, would be in a learning disabled class. Although the school officials have the legal authority to make placements, it is their usual practice to gain the approval of a student's parents before taking such an action. In this case, Billy's mother is adamantly against the idea. She says she does not want her child "in a class for criminals and dummies."

Questions to Consider

1. Should the counselor advocate that Billy be allowed to stay in the regular program? What reasons could be given to support this position?
2. The decision about Billy's placement aside, do you think that the counselor has any other ethical obligations related to the case?

CASE TWELVE: STUDENT WANTS INFORMATION ABOUT ABORTIONS

A 15-year-old student named Rachel comes to the counseling office seeking information about pregnancy and abortions. From the agitated manner in which she asks questions, the counselor thinks that in all likelihood Rachel is pregnant.

Questions to Consider

1. Should the counselor merely answer Rachel's questions, or should some further action be taken? What actions are called for and why are they indicated?
2. Is Rachel's age an important consideration in deciding how the counselor should respond to her? Why might it be significant?

CASE THIRTEEN: PARENT WANTS STUDENT IN ADVANCED PROGRAM

Michael is a 9th-grade student whose academic record has been about average. He does well in classes that he really enjoys, but less well when he is not excited about the subject matter. His mother requested that he be enrolled in the advanced mathematics program. The counselor is asked to check the records to determine if he could handle the work. The counselor concludes that the program would be a struggle, but Michael could probably handle it, if he made a maximum effort.

Questions to Consider

1. Should the counselor recommend that Michael be placed in the advanced program? What would be the reasons?
2. Should Michael's own view of the matter be given consideration? Should his view be the deciding factor? What would be the justification for this conclusion?

CASE FOURTEEN: COUNSELOR WANTS TO INITIATE A GROWTH GROUP

Ms. Atkinson is a counselor who has had much experience in group work, both as a member and as a leader. After working in a junior high school for 2 years, she decided that many of her 8th-grade girls shared similar problems and might benefit from a group experience. She proposed the idea of starting a group to the principal, who approved her plan. She sent out a form to parents explaining the goals and activities of the proposed program. The form included a place for parents to grant permission for their child to be included.

At the first meeting of the group, Ms. Atkinson explained the goals and the general group procedures. She also stressed the importance of confidentiality.

Shortly after the third weekly group meeting, Ms. Atkinson received a phone call from a mother of one of the group members. The mother was distressed because she had overheard her daughter and some of her friends discussing some personal information about the parents of another group member.

Questions to Consider

1. How should Ms. Atkinson respond to the parent's concerns?
2. Did Ms. Atkinson initiate the group in an ethically responsible way? What is the basis for this opinion?
3. Should group counseling take place in schools? What is the justification for providing it? What kinds of group counseling would be reasonable and which would not? How does the counselor make this choice?

CASE FIFTEEN: PRINCIPAL WANTS STUDENT REMOVED FROM PROGRAM

Charles is a 6th-grade student who has been to the counselor and the vice principal's office on many occasions. He has long been recognized as the class clown, but lately his antics have disrupted many groups and severely tested the patience of several instructors. The principal and the teachers involved want the school counselor to treat the student as incorrigible and take steps to remove him from regular classes. The counselor thinks that Charles has treatable psychological problems and removing him from the regular program would do him serious psychological and educational harm. At the end of a meeting of everyone with an interest in the case, the principal directs the counselor to initiate the paperwork to remove Charles from the regular program.

Questions to Consider

1. Should the counselor accept the decision of the principal and draw up the papers?
2. Would it be ethically justifiable for the counselor to meet with the parents to inform them about ways they could fight this action? If so, should the counselor merely provide information or advocate a certain approach? What would be the justification?

CASE SIXTEEN: STUDENT RESISTS REFERRAL

The counselor has good rapport with Mark, an 11th-grader. As they work together, it becomes apparent that there is a serious psychological problem behind his symptoms that the counselor lacks the training and the experience to treat. Mark is adamantly against the idea of a referral. He says he feels very comfortable with the school counselor and is unwilling to start a new relationship with another counselor. He says that he would rather have no counseling at all than begin working with someone else. Despite a lack of training, the counselor is likely to be of considerable help to him.

Questions to Consider

1. Should the counselor continue to work with Mark? Why or why not?
2. If the counselor decides to discontinue the relationship, how should it be terminated?

CASE SEVENTEEN: STUDENTS CLAIM THAT COUNSELOR'S COLLEAGUE IS BIASED

Ms. Lopez is a school counselor who is concerned by what students and some faculty are saying about her colleague, Mr. Martin. They say he is biased when he works with Hispanic students, and that he blames Hispanic clients for whatever problems they are experiencing. On the other hand, he is very sympathetic to the problems of his Anglo clients and often actively intervenes with faculty members on their behalf. They say that he encourages Anglo graduating seniors to apply to universities and colleges, whereas Hispanics are discouraged from continuing their education after high school or, at best, are directed toward vocational training programs.

Questions to Consider

1. Is the counselor ethically obligated to take some action in this situation? On what grounds should she intervene?
2. Should the counselor report what she has heard to the principal? What would be the justification?
3. Should the counselor inform Mr. Martin about the complaints against him? To what end should she pursue this line of action?

CASE EIGHTEEN: A LESBIAN STUDENT WORRIES ABOUT COMING OUT

Sixteen-year-old Martha tells the counselor she is a lesbian and does not know whether to tell her parents; they certainly will be shocked and probably not very supportive. Even more problematic is the question of whether to come out at school. Martha has a girlfriend and they both feel anxiety about keeping their relationship secret. Although they are mortified when straight students tell demeaning jokes about gays and lesbians, they feel they must remain silent. It's all getting to be too much to handle. Martha thinks she is about to have a nervous breakdown.

Questions to Consider

1. How might the counselor's own views—both descriptive (about what homosexuality is) and ethical—affect how counseling would be undertaken?
2. Are there circumstances in which the counselor should refer the case? If so, what kind of counselor?
3. Are there circumstances in which the counselor should attempt to establish gay and lesbian support groups in a school along the lines of Alateen or consciousness-raising groups for girls?
4. Does the counselor have any responsibility to combat homophobia among students and staff?

CASE NINETEEN: DRUG AND ALCOHOL USE AFFECTS STUDENT'S ACADEMIC PERFORMANCE

Bill, a 19-year-old, reports that he is using drugs and alcohol "just a little bit" and that this practice accounts for his deteriorating work in school. He is sure he can kick the habit by himself and requests that neither his teachers nor his parents be informed.

Questions to Consider

1. If you accept his plan, are you an enabler?
2. If Bill's marks return to normal, has the problem been solved? Is a decline in academic achievement not the problem but the symptom of a problem?
3. Should anyone be informed? If yes, who and for what purpose?

CHAPTER 9

Professional Ethics

In previous chapters, the discussion has focused on the many ethical problems that school counselors face and strategies for dealing with them. We have looked at situations in which the counselor deliberates and determines what to do in relative isolation. In addition, school counselors face ethical problems collectively, as members of a profession. This chapter explores what being "professional" means in this context.

WHAT IS A PROFESSION?

Despite many attempts, no standard definition of "profession" has emerged. Rich (1984) and others who have tried to identify a set of criteria to mark off this concept have relied heavily on an analysis of fields like medicine and law—the occupations most commonly recognized as professions. The lists of criteria vary somewhat but usually include the following:

1. A profession provides an important and unique service to society and requires considerable intellectual knowledge and skill to render.
2. The fundamental commitment of a profession is service to clients.
3. A profession promotes a broad range of autonomy for both the occupational group as a whole and the individual practitioner.
4. A profession has a comprehensive, self-governing organization that establishes standards of competency and ethics and practical guidelines for providing the service to the public.

The third characteristic in this list generates much controversy. Advocates for professions maintain that they cannot fulfill their fundamental commitment to serve clients without considerable individual and collective autonomy. Opponents are quick to point out cases of corruption—for example, when doctors or lawyers make personal gain their first priority. Critics maintain that the demand for autonomy is just an attempt to grab power; they claim that what professions are really after is less work, higher fees, and more of life's pleasures for their members.

One cannot deny that many in established professions have abused the considerable power their groups have secured. However, this may merely suggest a need for more careful scrutiny of, and more stringent controls on, the conduct of professionals. It is not sufficient grounds for concluding that professionalization is inherently corrupt. Let us look closer at the argument for professionalism.

WHY PROFESSIONALISM IS NEEDED

Suppose that a group of practitioners is committed to providing a vital service to the community and that the knowledge and skills essential to that end cannot be picked up easily on the job. They maintain that they need considerable autonomy for members individually, and for the group collectively, to maintain high standards of service. They argue that the demands of the job are complex, and the knowledge and skills needed to practice are sophisticated. Therefore, those in the occupational group are in the best position to:

1. Identify the specific services that the group can offer.
2. Determine what constitutes adequate preparation to offer the services.
3. Determine the conditions necessary for providing the services competently.
4. Establish standards of competence and ethics and use these to identify practitioners who are performing in an incompetent or unethical manner.

They maintain that a powerful organization is needed to enable the group to gain power and control and to ensure that they are used effectively and ethically. This organization would work to establish its own standards of competence and ethics to be adhered to wherever the service is offered. It would take measures to provide professionals with the conditions necessary to practice effectively, including guidelines regarding the relative importance of various services practitioners provide and what kind of preparation should be required to render them. It would decide what constitutes ethical conduct for its members, and it would assume responsibility for disciplining those found to be incompetent or unethical.

This line of thought suggests some desirable directions for the future of school counseling. The first consideration is to what extent school counseling can be described as a profession.

SCHOOL COUNSELING AS A PROFESSION

The first of the four criteria fits quite well. School counselors provide important services to students and their parents that cannot be provided adequately by others who work in the school community, such as teachers and administrators. School counselors may have a variety of duties, but they are usually consulted when a student exhibits social or psychological problems that are interfering with personal or academic development. Counselors assume major responsibility for identifying problems and devising plans for dealing with them. To provide these services effectively, they need considerable understanding of such things as the complex problems of urban life; the physical, psychological, and social development of children and adolescents; the dynamics of the family; the difficulties various individuals and groups experience in the complex social system of the school; how various psychological problems and learning disabilities can be overcome; and the ethical problems that commonly arise in the job. Becoming a competent school counselor requires considerable education, training, and supervised experience.

The second and third characteristics are not as easily applicable. School counselors have less professional autonomy than traditional professions like medicine, law, and private counseling. School counselors give their allegiance to a number of national professional organizations, but these groups have not had a major role in establishing the standards of competence and ethical conduct for the field. Requirements for entering the practice are, for the most part, established by state agencies. Policing the profession for incompetence and unethical conduct is left largely to school boards and the courts. Counseling organizations have not, as yet, had a major influence on the conduct of school counseling, though they do lobby state agencies and have formulated professional standards and codes of ethics.

The extent of a school counselor's autonomy varies considerably from community to community and school to school. There is often considerable confusion regarding the lines of authority for establishing school counseling regulations. Laws and school board policies establish part of the school counselor's obligations, but beyond that, guidelines governing daily activities may come from the superintendent's office, a central counseling office, or the principal.

LACK OF PROFESSIONALISM: THE PROBLEMS

Lack of the autonomy and leadership that could be provided by a powerful organization make it more difficult for school counselors to do their jobs effectively and ethically. Imagine a counselor who has just finished training and is strongly committed to serving clients. The counselor secures a position in a high school. A job description outlines the expectations of the position. It provides a general list of duties but does not indicate which takes priority over others, what decisions the new counselor will be expected to make, or what other demands may come from the school community.

Ill-Defined Responsibilities

As the school year begins, the counselor is given an extraordinary number of duties. There is much academic counseling with students and parents and providing information about postsecondary educational opportunities and careers. Many kinds of tests must be given and the results interpreted. There are often serious discipline cases to be handled. The principal asks the counselor to initiate a program to ease racial and ethnic tensions. There are administrative chores like student placement and schedule making. An administrator and some teachers want a troublesome student removed. A parent wants a child enrolled in a special program even though the child is not qualified. When time allows for the kind of counseling for which the counselor was trained, others in the school community have strong opinions to express.

It does not take long to discover that much time is spent on routine counseling tasks and that the counselor's expertise is often ignored when important decisions are made. Many obstacles interfere with the counselor's commitment to render service to clients.

Unhelpful Codes of Ethics

There are complex cases to handle, like those presented in previous chapters. A clearer idea of legal and ethical limits is needed. Reading school board publications, reviewing laws related to counseling, and talking to colleagues are of some help to counselors. However, laws, court decisions, and school board policies are often confusing and indecisive when applied to specific situations. They often seem well justified when applied to the school population in general, but not necessarily with individuals in trouble. On occasion, a directive from one of these sources may do more harm than good to a client.

A number of cases present ethical problems, such as that of confidentiality. A 9th-grade boy reveals something his parents would likely want to know: Would breaking confidentiality be justified? The "Ethical Standards for School Counselors" is specifically designed to help deal with ethical problems (see Appendix B). However, the principles tend to be platitudinous and subject to a wide variety of interpretations. For example, the school counselor:

1. Has a primary obligation and loyalty to the pupil, who is to be treated with respect as a unique individual. (A.1)
2. Protects the confidentiality of information received in the counseling process as specified by law and ethical standards. (A.8)
3. Provides parents with accurate, comprehensive, and relevant information in an objective and caring manner. (B.3)

The first principle obliges the counselor to put loyalty to pupils first, but what loyalty compels one to do and what its limits are is left unclear. Would it bind Ms. Larkin to keep Maria's pregnancy a secret from her parents? Would it necessitate that Jennifer's counselor stand aside as Jennifer leaves to join her boyfriend? Presumably, the counselor also has some obligation to be loyal to parents, administrators, and teachers, or are clients the only ones "to be treated with respect as unique individuals"? Counselors have serious problems when they try to juggle accountability to students, teachers, and parents, but precepts like these are not much help.

The second principle, A.8, tells the counselor to obey the law and be guided by professional standards in deciding matters of confidentiality. (It does not suggest where counselors can find these professional standards. One might expect a document entitled "Ethical Standards for School Counselors" to provide them.) Would this principle help Mr. Thompson decide whether or not to call a child protection agency? Might actions required by professional standards ever violate the law? For example, counselors on occasion have refused to report suspicions of child abuse as mandated by law because in their judgment it would do more harm than good. If there is a conflict, this principle does not help the counselor to decide whether "obeying the law" or "acting according to ethical principles" is the higher obligation.

The manner in which counselors should provide information to parents is described in B.3, but this precept avoids a much more important question. Whereas A.8 suggests that counselors are obliged to honor the confidentiality of their clients, B.3 states that they are compelled to share some information with parents. It is not uncommon for school counselors to have great difficulty deciding just what to divulge and what to withhold. Would these principles help Ms. Larkin, Ms. Hahn, or Jennifer's counselor decide what to disclose to their clients' families?

Of course, new counselors should not expect a code of ethics to spell out what they should and should not do in all situations. The ethical problems of school counseling are often too complex, and the circumstances in which problems arise can vary greatly. But surely, they should be able to expect more help than these principles provide as they struggle with difficult ethical problems.

Lack of Autonomy

The areas of authority and responsibility for school counselors are unclear, and counselors lack the autonomy to make important decisions. As professionals, they should have a major role in determining what kinds of counseling programs the school will be offering, who should be accepted for these programs, how counseling should be conducted, and what administrators and faculty will be allowed to ask of them. In most cases, counselor and client should decide what actions to take to address the problem. These are ethical issues because the first duty of a member of a profession is to render competent service to clients. If there are conditions that interfere with acting on this commitment, professionals are ethically obligated to do what they reasonably can to alleviate them. Professionals cannot ethically resign themselves to the situation, shrug their shoulders and sigh, "You can't buck the system." Some reasonable actions that may be taken follow:

1. Meet with other school counselors on a regular basis. Establish, as specifically as possible, what constitutes competent and ethical school counseling and the school conditions that are necessary for an effective program. Identify obstacles and discuss how they might be overcome.
2. Meet with the administrators, faculty, and parents at the school to talk about ways to improve the counseling program. Discuss such matters as what kinds of problems are appropriate for counseling, how counseling should be made available to clients, what

information should be kept confidential, and what kinds of reports parents and teachers should be given. Clear guidelines should be established.

We have noted throughout this book that school counselors work in a complex social system and are subject to a variety of pressures. They are expected to act in accordance with laws and school board policies. Administrators, teachers, and parents are likely to have definite ideas about their role. In this setting, they must make their own judgments regarding ethical obligations to the school community and their clients.

THE ROLE OF PROFESSIONAL ORGANIZATIONS

These problems are ones that most school counselors face. However, a strong, cohesive organization could do much to improve the situation for counselors at the local level. To help them provide services to their clients in an effective and ethical manner, a national organization could take the following steps:

1. Work to clarify the role of the school counselor. Determine which of the many kinds of tasks they perform are the essential ones that define the role.
2. Decide what preparation is needed to perform these tasks competently and ethically. Consider such questions as what knowledge and skills are required, what kinds of examinations, and how much supervised internship.
3. Determine what conditions at schools are essential for providing an effective counseling program. Consider such questions as what kind of authority counselors need, how their responsibilities can best be coordinated with those of teachers, where and when counseling should take place, and how clients should be selected.
4. Develop a code of ethics clearly derived from fundamental ethical principles—respect for persons, maximization of freedom, consideration of interests, and equality. Make sure the principles are stated clearly enough to be connected to specific actions in particular circumstances. Analyze ethical dilemmas that are common in school counseling, and identify the conflicts among the principles that underlie them. Try to determine which principles take priority under various sets of circumstances. Continually revise and refine the principles by considering their application

to difficult cases. Publish a casebook with analyses so that members can benefit from the collective thinking of the organization.

We recognize that these tasks are just preliminary. Once those within the ranks reach an agreement regarding the essentials of a school counseling program and what constitutes competent and ethical conduct for counselors, they face the political task of establishing standards across the country.

A more formidable undertaking, which is sorely needed, is the reform of school counseling programs to provide those in training with the ethical tools to interpret ethical codes intelligently and to make wise decisions in cases that the codes do not cover. This reform would add substance to the claim that school counseling has become a profession.

APPENDIX A

Ethical Standards of the American Counseling Association*

Preamble

The Association is an educational, scientific, and professional organization whose members are dedicated to the enhancement of each individual and thus to the service of society.

The association recognizes that the role definitions and work settings of its members include a wide variety of academic disciplines, levels of academic preparation, and agency services. This diversity reflects the breadth of the Association's interest and influence. It also poses challenging complexities in efforts to set standards for the performance of members, desired requisite preparation or practice, and supporting social, legal, and ethical controls.

The specification of ethical standards enables the Association to clarify to present and future members the nature of ethical responsibilities held in common by its members.

The existence of such standards serves to stimulate greater concern by its members for their own professional functioning and for the conduct of fellow professionals such as counselors, guidance and student personnel workers, and others in the helping professions. As the ethical code of the Association, this document establishes principles that define the ethical behavior of Association members. Additional ethical guidelines developed by the Association's Divisions for their specialty areas may further define a member's ethical behavior.

Section A: General

1. The member influences the development of the profession by continuous efforts to improve professional practices, teaching, services,

*Revised March 1988 by American Counseling Association, Alexandria, VA.

and research. Professional growth is continuous throughout the member's career and is exemplified by the development of a philosophy that explains how and why a member functions in the helping relationship. Members must gather data on their effectiveness and be guided by the findings. Members recognize the need for continuous education to ensure competent service.

2. The member has a responsibility both to the individual who is served and to the institution within which the service is performed to maintain high standards of professional conduct. The member strives to maintain the highest levels of professional services offered to the individuals to be served. The member also strives to assist the agency, organization, or institution in providing the highest caliber of professional services. The acceptance of employment in an institution implies that the member is in agreement with the general policies and principles of the institution. Therefore the professional activities of the member are also in accord with the objectives of the institution. If, despite concerted efforts, the member cannot reach agreement with the employer as to the acceptable standards of conduct that allow for changes in institutional policy conducive to the positive growth and development of clients, then terminating the affiliation should be seriously considered.

3. Ethical behavior among professional associates, both members and nonmembers, must be expected at all times. When information is possessed that raises doubt as to the ethical behavior of professional colleagues, whether Association members or not, the member must take action to attempt to rectify such a condition. Such action shall use the institution's channels first and then use the procedures established by the Association.

4. The member neither claims nor implies professional qualifications exceeding those possessed and is responsible for correcting any misrepresentations of these qualifications by others.

5. In established fees for professional counseling services, members must consider the financial status of clients and locality. In the event that the established fee structure is inappropriate for a client, assistance must be provided in finding comparable services at an acceptable cost.

6. When members provide information to the public or to subordinates, peers, or supervisors, they have a responsibility to ensure that the content is general, unidentified client information that is accurate, unbiased, and consists of objective, factual data.

7. Members recognize their boundaries of competence and provide only those services and use only those techniques for which they were qualified by training or experience. Members should only accept those positions for which they are professionally qualified.

8. In the counseling relationship, the counselor is aware of the intimacy of the relationship and maintains respect for the client and avoids engaging in activities that seek to meet the counselor's personal needs at the expense of the client.

9. Members do not condone or engage in sexual harassment, which is defined as deliberate or repeated comments, gestures, or physical contacts of a sexual nature.

10. The member avoids bringing personal issues into the counseling relationship, especially if the potential for harm is present. Through awareness of the negative impact of both racial and sexual stereotyping and discrimination, the counselor guards the individual rights and personal dignity of the client in the counseling relationship.

11. Products or services provided by the member by means of classsroom instruction, public lectures, demonstrations, written articles, radio or television programs, or other types of media must meet the criteria cited in these standards.

Section B: Counseling Relationships

This section refers to practices and procedures of individual and/or group counseling relationships.

The member must recognize the need for client freedom of choice. Under those circumstances where this is not possible, the member must apprise the client of restrictions that may limit their freedom of choice.

1. The member's primary obligation is to respect the integrity and promote the welfare of client(s), whether the client(s) is (are) assisted individually or in a group relationship. In a group setting, the member is also responsible for taking reasonable precautions to protect individuals from physical and/or psychological trauma resulting from interaction with the group.

2. Members make provisions for maintaining confidentiality in the storage and disposal of records that follow an established record retention and disposition policy. The counseling relationship and information resulting therefrom must be kept confidential, consistent with the obligations of the member as a professional person. In a group counseling setting, the counselor must set a norm of confidentiality regarding all group participants' disclosures.

3. If an individual is already in a counseling relationship with another professional person, the member does not enter into a counseling relationship without first contacting and receiving the approval of that other professional. If the member discovers that the client is in another counseling relationship after the counseling relationship be-

gins, the member must gain the consent of the other professional or terminate the relationship, unless the client elects to terminate the other relationship.

4. When the client's conditions indicates that there is clear and imminent danger to the client or others, the member must take reasonable personal action or inform responsible authorities. Consultation with other professionals must be used where possible. The assumption or responsibility for the client's(s') behavior must be taken only after careful deliberation. The client must be involved in the resumption of responsibility as quickly as possible.

5. Records of the counseling relationship, including interview notes, test data, correspondence, tape recording, electronic data storage, and other documents are to be considered a part of the records of the institution or agency in which the counselor is employed unless specified by state statute or regulation. Revelation to others of counseling material must occur only upon the expressed consent of the client.

6. In view of the extensive data storage and processing capacities of the computer, the member must ensure that data maintained in a computer is: (a) limited to information that is appropriate and necessary for the services being provided; (b) destroyed after it is determined that the information is no longer of any value in providing services; and (c) restricted in terms of access to appropriate staff members involved in the provision of services by using the best computer security methods available.

7. Use of data derived from a counseling relationship for purposes of counselor training or research shall be confined to content that can be disguised to insure full protection of the identity of the subject client.

8. The member must inform the client of the purposes, goals, techniques, rules of procedure, and limitations that may affect the relationship at or before the time that the counseling relationship is entered. When working with minors or persons who are unable to give consent, the member protects these clients' best interests.

9. In view of the common misconceptions related to the perceived inherent validity of computer-generated data and narrative reports, the member must ensure that the client is provided with information as part of the counseling relationship that adequately explains the limitations of computer technology.

10. The member must screen prospective group participants, especially when the emphasis is on self-understanding and growth through self-disclosure. The member must maintain an awareness of the group participants' compatibility throughout the life of the group.

11. The member may choose to consult with any other profession-

ally competent person about a client. In choosing a consultant, the member must avoid placing the consultant in a conflict of interest situation that would preclude the consultant's being a proper party to the member's efforts to help the client.

12. If the member determines an inability to be of professional assistance to the client, the member must either avoid initiating the counseling relationship or immediately terminate that relationship. In either event, the member must suggest appropriate alternatives. (The member must be knowledgeable about referral resources so that a satisfactory referral can be initiated.) In the event the client declines the suggested referral, the member is not obligated to continue the relationship.

13. When the member has other relationships, particularly of an administrative, supervisory, and /or evaluative nature with an individual seeking counseling services, the member must not serve as the counselor but should refer the individual to another professional. Only in instances where such an alternative is unavailable and where the individual's situation warrants counseling intervention should the member enter into and/or maintain a counseling relationship. Dual relationships with clients that might impair the member's objectivity and professional judgment (e.g., as with close friends or relatives) must be avoided and/or the counseling relationship terminated through referral to another competent professional.

14. The member will avoid any type of sexual intimacies with clients. Sexual relationships with clients are unethical.

15. All experimental methods of treatment must be clearly indicated to prospective recipients, and safety precautions are to be adhered to by the member.

16. When computer applications are used as a component of counseling services, the member must ensure that: (a) the client is intellectually, emotionally, and physically capable of using the computer application; (b) the computer application is appropriate for the needs of the client; (c) the client understands the purpose and operation of the computer application; and (d) a followup of client use of a computer application is provided to both correct possible problems (misconceptions or inappropriate use) and assess subsequent needs.

17. When the member is engaged in short-term group treatment/ training programs (e.g., marathons and other encounter-type or growth groups), the member ensures that there is professional assistance available during and following the group experience.

18. Should the member be engaged in a work setting that calls for any variation from the above statements, the member is obligated to

consult with other professionals whenever possible to consider justifiable alternatives.

19. The member must ensure that members of various ethnic, racial, religious, disability, and socioeconomic groups have equal access to computer applications used to support counseling services and that the content of available computer applications does not discriminate against the groups described above.

20. When computer applications are developed by the member for use by the general public as self-help/stand-alone computer software, the member must ensure that: (a) self-help computer applications are designed from the beginning to function in a stand-alone manner as opposed to modifying software that was originally designed to require support from a counselor; (b) self-help computer applications will include within the program statements regarding intended user outcomes, suggestions for using the software, a description of the conditions under which self-help computer applications might not be appropriate, and a description of when and how counseling services might be beneficial; and (c) the manual for such applications will include the qualifications of the developer, the developmental process, validation data, and operating procedures.

Section C: Measurement and Evaluation

The primary purpose of educational and psychological testing is to provide descriptive measures that are objective and interpretable in either comparative or absolute terms. The member must recognize the need to interpret the statements that follow as applying to the whole range of appraisal techniques including test and nontest data. Test results constitute only one of a variety of pertinent sources of information for personnel, guidance, and counseling decisions.

1. The member must provide specific orientation or information to the examinee(s) prior to and following the test administration so that the results of testing may be placed in proper perspective with other relevant factors. In so doing, the member must recognize the effects of socioeconomic, ethnic, and cultural factors in test scores. It is the member's professional responsibility to use additional unvalidated information carefully in modifying interpretation of the test results.

2. In selecting tests for use in a given situation or with a particular client, the member must consider carefully the specific validity, reliability, and appropriateness of the test(s). General validity, reliability, and related issues may be questioned legally as well as ethically when tests

are used for vocational and educational selection, placement, or counseling.

3. When making any statement to the public about tests and testing, the member must give accurate information and avoid false claims or misconceptions. Special efforts are often required to avoid unwarranted connotations of such terms as IQ and grade equivalent scores.

4. Different tests demand different levels of competence for administration, scoring, and interpretation. Members must recognize the limits of their competence and perform only those functions for which they are prepared. In particular, members using computer-based test interpretations must be trained in the construct being measured and the specific instrument being used prior to using this type of computer application.

5. In situations where a computer is used for test administration and scoring, the member is responsible for ensuring that administration and scoring programs function properly to provide clients with accurate test results.

6. Tests must be administered under the same conditions that were established in their standardization. When tests are not administered under standard conditions or when unusual behavior or irregularities occur during the testing session, those conditions must be noted and the results designated as invalid or of questionable validity. Unsupervised or inadequately supervised test-taking, such as the use of tests through the mails, is considered unethical. On the other hand, the use of instruments that are so designed or standardized to be self-administered and self-scored, such as interest inventories, is to be encouraged.

7. The meaningfulness of test results used in personnel, guidance, and counseling functions generally depends on the examinee's unfamiliarity with the specific items on the test. Any prior coaching or dissemination of the test materials can invalidate test results. Therefore, test security is one of the professional obligations of the member. Conditions that produce most favorable test results must be made known to the examinee.

8. The purpose of testing and the explicit use of the results must be made known to the examinee prior to testing. The counselor must ensure that instrument limitations are not exceeded and that periodic review and/or retesting are made to prevent client stereotyping.

9. The examinee's welfare and explicit prior understanding must be the criteria for determining the recipients of the test results. The member must see that specific interpretation accompanies any release of individual or group test data. The interpretation of test data must be related to the examinee's particular concerns.

10. Members responsible for making decisions based on test results have an understanding to educational and psychological measurement, validation criteria, and test research.

11. The member must be cautious when interpreting the results of research instruments possessing insufficient technical data. The specific purposes for the use of such instrument must be stated explicitly to examinees.

12. The member must proceed with caution when attempting to evaluate and interpret the performance of minority group members or other persons who are not represented in the norm group on which the instrument was standardized.

13. When computer-based test interpretations are developed by the member to support the assessment process, the member must ensure that the validity of such interpretations is established prior to the commercial distribution of such a computer application.

14. The member recognizes that test results may become obsolete. The member will avoid and prevent the misuse of obsolete test results.

15. The member must guard against the appropriation, reproduction, or modification of published tests or parts thereof without acknowledgment and permission from the previous publisher.

16. Regarding the preparation, publication, and distribution of tests, reference should be made to:

a. "Standards for Educational and Psychological Testing," revised edition, 1985, published by the American Psychological Association on behalf of itself, the American Educational Research Association, and the National Council of Measurement in Education.
b. "The Responsible Use of Tests: A Position Paper of AMEG, APGA, and NCME." *Measurement and Evaluation in Guidance*. 1972, pp. 385–388.
c. "Responsibilities of Users of Standardized Tests." APGA, *Guidepost*. October 5, 1978, pp. 5–8.

Section D: Research and Publication

1. Guidelines on research with human subjects should be adhered to, such as:

a. *Ethical Principles in the Conduct of Research with Human Participants*, Washington, D.C.: American Psychological Association, Inc., 1982.
b. Code of Federal Regulation, Title 45, Subtitle A, Pan 46, as currently issued.

c. *Ethical Principles of Psychologists*, American Psychological Association, Inc. Principle #9: Research with Human Participants.
d. Family Educational Rights and Privacy Act (the Buckley Amendment).
e. Current federal regulations and various state rights privacy acts.

2. In planning any research activity dealing with human subjects, the member must be aware of and responsive to all pertinent ethical principles and ensure that the research problem, design, and execution are in full compliance with them.

3. Responsibility for ethical research practice lies with principal researcher while others involved in the research activities share ethical obligation and full responsibility for their own actions.

4. In research with human subjects, researchers are responsible for the subjects' welfare throughout the experiment, and they must take all reasonable precautions to avoid causing injurious psychological, physical, or social effects on their subjects.

5. All research subjects must be informed of the purpose of the study except when withholding information or providing misinformation to them is essential to the investigation. In such research, the member must be responsible for corrective action as soon as possible following completion of the research.

6. Participation in research must be voluntary. Involuntary participation is appropriate only when it can be demonstrated that participation will have no harmful effects on subjects and is essential to the investigation.

7. When reporting research results, explicit mention must be made of all variables and conditions known to the investigator that might affect the outcome of the investigation or the interpretation of data.

8. The member must be responsible for conducting and reporting investigations in a manner that minimizes the possibility that results will be misleading.

9. The member has an obligation to make available sufficient original research data to qualified others who may wish to replicate the study.

10. When supplying data, aiding in the research of another person, reporting research results, or making original data available, due care must be taken to disguise the identity of the subjects in the absence of specific authorization from such subjects to do otherwise.

11. When conducting and reporting research, the member must be familiar with and give recognition to previous work on the topic, as well as to observe all copyright laws and follow the principles of giving full credit to all to whom credit is due.

12. The member must give due credit through joint authorship, acknowledgments, footnote statements, or other appropriate means to those who have contributed significantly to the research and/or publication, in accordance with such contributions.

13. The member must communicate to other members the result of any research judged to be of professional or scientific value. Results reflecting unfavorably on institutions, programs, services, or vested interests must not be withheld for such reasons.

14. If members agree to cooperate with another individual in research and/or publication, they incur an obligation to cooperate as promised in terms of punctuality of performance and with full regard to the completeness and accuracy of the information required.

15. Ethical practice requires that authors not submit the same manuscript or one essentially similar in content for simultaneous publication consideration by two or more journals. In addition, manuscripts published in whole or in substantial part in another journal or published work should not be submitted for publication without acknowledgment and permission from the previous publication.

Section E: Consulting

Consultation refers to a voluntary relationship between a professional helper and help-needing individual, group, or social unit in which the consultant is providing help to the client(s) in defining and solving a work-related problem or potential problem with a client or client system.

1. The member acting as consultant must have a high degree of self-awareness of his/her own values, knowledge, skills, limitations, and needs in entering a helping relationship that involves human and/or organizational change and that the focus of the relationship be on the issues to be resolved and not on the person(s) presenting the problem.

2. There must be understanding and agreement between member and client for the problem definition, change of goals, and prediction of consequences of interventions selected.

3. The member must be reasonably certain that she/he or the organization represented has the necessary competencies and resources for giving the kind of help that is needed now or may be needed later and that appropriate referral resources are available to the consultant.

4. The consulting relationship must be one in which client adaptability and growth toward self-direction are encouraged and cultivated. The member must maintain this role consistently and not become a decision maker for the client or create a future dependency on the consultant.

5. When announcing consultant availability for services, the member conscientiously adheres to the Association's Ethical Standards.

6. The member must refuse a private fee or other remuneration for consultation with persons who are entitled to those services through the member's employing institution or agency. The policies of a particular agency may make explicit provisions for private practice with agency clients by members of its staff. In such instances, the clients must be apprised of other options open to them should they seek private counseling services.

Section F: Private Practice

1. The member should assist the profession by facilitating the availability of counseling services in private as well as public settings.

2. In advertising services as a private practitioner, the member must advertise the services in a manner that accurately informs the public of professional services, expertise, and techniques of counseling available. A member who assumes an executive leadership role in the organization shall not permit his/her name to be used in professional notices during periods when he/she is not actively engaged in the private practice of counseling.

3. The member may list the following: highest advanced degree, type and level of certification and/or license, address, telephone number, office hours, type and/or description of services, and other related information. Such information must not contain false, inaccurate, misleading, partial, out-of-context, or deceptive material or statements.

4. Members do not present their affiliations with any organization in such a way that would imply inaccurate sponsorship or certification by that organization.

5. Members may join in partnership/corporation with other members and/or other professionals provided that each member of the partnership or corporation makes clear the separate specialties by name in compliance with the regulations of the locality.

6. A member has an obligation to withdraw from a counseling relationship if it is believed that employment will result in violation of the Ethical Standards. If the mental or physical condition of the member renders it difficult to carry out an effective professional relationship, or if the member is discharged by the client because the counseling relationship is no longer productive for the client, then the member is obligated to terminate the counseling relationship.

7. A member must adhere to the regulations for private practice of the locality where the services are offered.

8. It is unethical to use one's institutional affiliation to recruit clients for one's private practice.

Section G: Personnel Administration

It is recognized that most members are employed in public or quasi-public institutions. The functioning of a member within an institution must contribute to the goals of the institution and vice versa if either is to accomplish their respective goals or objectives. It is therefore essential that the member and the institution function in ways to: (a) make the institutional goals specific and public; (b) make the member's contribution to institutional goals specific; and (c) foster mutual accountability for goal achievement.

To accomplish these objectives, it is recognized that the member and the employer must share responsibilities in the formulation and implementation of personnel policies.

1. Members must define and describe the parameters and levels of their professional competency.

2. Members must establish interpersonal relations and working agreements with supervisors and subordinates regarding counseling or clinical relationships, confidentiality, distinction between public and private material, maintenance and dissemination of recorded information, work load, and accountability. Working agreement in each instance must be specified and made known to those concerned.

3. Members must alert their employers to conditions that may be potentially disruptive or damaging.

4. Members must inform employers of conditions that may limit their effectiveness.

5. Members must submit regularly to professional review and evaluation.

6. Members must be responsible for inservice development of self and/or staff.

7. Members must inform their staff of goals and programs.

8. Members must provide personnel practices that guarantee and enhance the right and welfare of each recipient of their service.

9. Members must select competent persons and assign responsibilities compatible with their skills and experiences.

10. The member, at the onset of a counseling relationship, will inform the client of the member's intended use of supervisors regarding the disclosure of information concerning this case. The member will clearly inform the client of the limits of confidentiality in the relationship.

11. Members, as either employers or employees, do not engage in

or condone practices that are inhumane, illegal, or unjustifiable (such as considerations based on sex, handicap, age, race) in hiring, promotions, or training.

Section H: Preparation Standards

Members who are responsible for training others must be guided by the preparation standards of the Association and relevant Division(s). The member who functions in the capacity of trainer assumes unique ethical responsibilities that frequently go beyond that of the member who does not function in a training capacity. These ethical responsibilities are outlined as follows:

1. Members must orient student to program expectations, basic skills development, and employment prospects prior to admission to the program.
2. Members in charge of learning experiences must establish programs that integrate academic study and supervised practice.
3. Members must establish a program directed toward developing students' skills, knowledge, and self-understanding stated whenever possible in competency or performance terms.
4. Members must identify the levels of competencies of their student in compliance with relevant Division standards. These competencies must accommodate the paraprofessional as well as the professional.
5. Members, through continual student evaluation and appraisal, must be aware of the personal limitations of the learner that might impede future performance. The instructor must not only assist the learner in securing remedial assistance but also screen from the program those individuals who are unable to provide competent services.
6. Members must provide a program that includes training in research commensurate with levels of role functioning. Paraprofessional and technician-level personnel must be trained as consumers of research. In addition, personnel must learn how to evaluate their own and their program's effectiveness. Graduate training, especially at the doctoral level, would include preparation for original research by the member.
7. Members must make students aware of the ethical responsibilities and standards of the profession.
8. Preparatory programs must encourage students to value the ideals of service to individuals and to society. In this regard, direct financial remuneration or lack thereof must not be allowed to overshadow professional and humanitarian need.
9. Members responsible for educational programs must be skilled as teachers and practitioners.

10. Members must present thoroughly varied theoretical positions so that students may make comparisons and have the opportunity to select a position.

11. Members must develop clear policies within their institutions regarding field placement and the roles of the student and the instructor in such placement.

12. Members must ensure that forms of learning focusing on self-understanding or growth are voluntary, or if required as part of the educational program, are made known to prospective students prior to entering the program. When the educational program offers a growth experience with an emphasis on self-disclosure or other relatively intimate or personal involvement, the member must have no administrative, supervisory, or evaluating authority regarding the participant.

13. The member will at all times provide students with clear and equally acceptable alternatives for self-understanding or growth experiences. The member will assure students that they have a right to accept these alternatives without prejudice or penalty.

14. Members must conduct an educational program in keeping with the current relevant guidelines of the Association.

APPENDIX B

Ethical Standards of the American School Counselor Association*

Preamble

The American School Counselor Association is a professional organization whose members have a unique and distinctive preparation, grounded in the behavioral sciences, with training in clinical skills adapted to the school setting. School counselors subscribe to the following basic tenets of the counseling process from which professional responsibilities are derived:

1. Each person has the right to respect and dignity as a human being and to counseling services without prejudice as to person, character, belief or practice.
2. Each person has the right to self-direction and self-development.
3. Each person has the right of choice and the responsibility for decisions reached.
4. The counselor assists in the growth and development of each individual and uses his/her highly specialized skills to ensure that the rights of the counselee are properly protected within the structure of the school program.
5. The counselor-client relationship is private and thereby requires compliance with all laws, policies and ethical standards pertaining to confidentiality.

In this document, the American School Counselor Association has identified the standards of conduct necessary to maintain and regulate the high standards of integrity and leadership among its members. The Association recognizes the basic commitment of its members to the Ethical Standards of its parent organization, the American Association for

*Revised March 1984, by the American School Counselor Association, Alexandria, VA.

Counseling and Development, and nothing in this document shall be construed to supplant the code. The Ethical Standards for School Counselors was developed to complement the AACD standards by clarifying the nature of ethical responsibilities of counselors in the school setting. The purposes of this document are to:

1. Serve as a guide for the ethical practices of all school counselors regardless of level, area, or population served.

2. Provide benchmarks for both self-appraisal and peer evaluations regarding counselor responsibilities to pupils, parents, professional colleagues, school and community, self, and the counseling profession.

3. Inform those served by the school counselor of acceptable counselor practices and expected professional deportment.

A. Responsibilities to Pupils

The school counselor:

1. Has a primary obligation and loyalty to the pupil, who is to be treated with respect as a unique individual.

2. Is concerned with the total needs of the pupil (educational, vocational, personal and social) and encourages the maximum growth and development of each counselee.

3. Informs the counselee of the purposes, goals, techniques, and rules of procedure under which she/he may receive counseling assistance at or before the time when the counseling relationship is entered. Prior notice includes the possible necessity for consulting with other professionals, privileged communication, and legal or other authoritative restraints.

4. Refrains from consciously encouraging the counselee's acceptance of values, lifestyles, plans, decisions, and beliefs that represent only the counselor's personal orientation.

5. Is responsible for keeping abreast of laws relating to pupils and ensures that the rights of pupils are adequately provided for and protected.

6. Makes appropriate referrals when professional assistance can no longer be provided to the counselee. Appropriate referral necessitates knowledge about available resources.

7. Protects the confidentiality of pupil records and releases personal data only according to prescribed laws and school policies. The counselor shall provide an accurate, objective, and appropriately detailed interpretation of pupil information.

8. Protects the confidentiality of information received in the counseling process as specified by law and ethical standards.

9. Informs the appropriate authorities when the counselee's conditions indicates a clear and imminent danger to the counselee or others. This is to be done after deliberation and, where possible, after consultation with other professionals.

10. Provides explanations of the nature, purposes, and results of tests in language that is understandable to the client(s).

11. Adheres to the relevant standards regarding selection, administration, and interpretation of assessment techniques.

B. Responsibilities to Parents

The school counselor:

1. Respects the inherent rights and responsibilities of parents for their children and endeavors to establish a cooperative relationship with parents to facilitate the maximum development of the counselee.

2. Informs parents of the counselor's role with emphasis on the confidential nature of the counseling relationship between the counselor and counselee.

3. Provides parents with accurate, comprehensive and relevant information in an objective and caring manner.

4. Treats information received from parents in a confidential and appropriate manner.

5. Shares information about a counselee only with those persons properly authorized to receive such information.

6. Follows local guidelines when assisting parents experiencing family difficulties which interfere with the counselee's effectiveness and welfare.

C. Responsibilities to Colleagues and Professional Associates

The school counselor:

1. Establishes and maintains a cooperative relationship with faculty, staff, and administration to facilitate the provision of optimum guidance and counseling services.

2. Promotes awareness and adherence to appropriate guidelines regarding confidentiality, the distinction between public and private information, and staff consultation.

3. Treats colleagues with respect, courtesy, fairness, and good faith. The qualifications, views, and findings of colleagues are represented accurately and fairly to enhance the image of competent professionals.

4. Provides professional personnel with accurate, objective, concise and meaningful data necessary to adequately evaluate, counsel and assist the counselee.

5. Is aware of and fully utilizes related professions and organizations to whom the counselee may be referred.

D. Responsibilities to the School and Community

The school counselor:

1. Supports and protects the educational program against any infringement not in the best interest of pupils.
2. Informs appropriate officials of conditions that may be potentially disruptive or damaging to the school's mission, personnel, and property.
3. Delineates and promotes the counselor's role and function in meeting the needs of those served. The counselor will notify appropriate school officials of conditions which may limit or curtail their effectiveness in providing services.
4. Assists in the development of (1) curricular and environmental conditions appropriate for the school and community, (2) educational procedures and programs to meet pupil needs, and (3) a systematic evaluation process for guidance and counseling programs, services and personnel.
5. Works cooperatively with agencies, organizations, and individuals in the school and community without regard to personal reward or remuneration.

E. Responsibilities to Self

The school counselor:

1. Functions within the boundaries of individual professional competence and accepts responsibility for the consequences of his/her actions.
2. Is aware of the potential effects of personal characteristics on services to clients.
3. Monitors personal functioning and effectiveness and refrains from any activity likely to lead to inadequate professional services or harm to a client.
4. Strives through personal initiative to maintain professional competence and keep abreast of innovations and trends in the profession.

F. Responsibilities to the Profession

The school counselor:

1. Conducts herself/himself in such a manner as to bring credit to self and the profession.

2. Conducts appropriate research and reports findings in a manner consistent with acceptable educational and psychological research practices.

3. Actively participates in local, state, and national associations which foster the development and improvement of school counseling.

4. Adheres to ethical standards of the profession, other official policy statements pertaining to counseling, and relevant statutes established by federal, state and local governments.

5. Clearly distinguishes between statements and actions made as a private individual and as a representative of the school counseling profession.

G. Maintenance of Standards

Ethical behavior among professional school counselors is expected at all times. When there exists serious doubt as to the ethical behavior of colleagues, or if counselors are forced to work in situations or abide by policies which do not reflect the standards as outlined in these Ethical Standards for School Counselors or the AACD Ethical Standards, the counselor is obligated to take appropriate action to rectify the condition. The following procedures may serve as a guide:

1. The counselor shall utilize the channels established within the school and/or system. This may include both informal and formal procedures.

2. If the matter remains unresolved, referral for review and appropriate action should be made to the Ethics Committees in the following sequence: local counselor association, state counselor association, national counselor association.

Bibliography

Abeles, N. (1980). Teaching ethical principles by means of value confrontations. *Psychotherapy: Theory, Research and Practice, 17*(4), 384–391.

American Personnel and Guidance Association. (1990). *Ethical standards casebook* (4th ed.). Falls Church, VA: Author.

Applebaum, P. S. (1985). *Tarasoff* and the clinician: The problem in fulfilling the duty to protect. *American Journal of Psychiatry, 142*(4), 425–429.

Aristotle. (1980). *Nicomachean ethics* (W. D. Ross, Trans.). New York: Oxford University Press.

Arrington, R. L. (1978). On respect. *Journal of Value Inquiry, 12*(1), 1–12.

Arthur, G. L. (1993). *Confidentiality and privileged communication*. Alexandria, VA: American Counseling Association.

Ayer, A. J. (1953). *Language, truth, and logic* (2nd ed.). London: Gollancz.

Baier, K. (1965). *The moral point of view*. New York: Random House.

Benn, S. I. (1975/1976). Freedom, autonomy and the concept of a person. *Proceedings of the Aristotelian Society* (New Series), *76*, 109–130.

Benn, S. I. (1980). Privacy and respect for persons: A reply. *Australian Journal of Philosophy, 58*, 54–61.

Berlin, I. (1969). *Four essays on liberty*. London: Oxford University Press.

Bersoff, D. N. (1975). Professional ethics and legal responsibilities: On the horns of a dilemma. *Journal of School Psychology, 13*(4), 359–376.

Biggs, D. A., & Blocher, D. (1987). *Foundations of ethical counseling*. New York: Springer.

Bowman, J., & Reeves, T. G. (1987). Moral development and empathy in counseling. *Counselor Education and Supervision, 26*(4), 293–298.

Breggin, P. R. (1971). Psychotherapy as applied ethics. *Psychiatry, 34*(1), 59–74.

Buber, M. (1957). Guilt and guilt feelings. *Psychiatry, 20*, 114–129.

Burke, M. T., & Miranti, J. G. (1992). *Ethical and spiritual values in counseling*. Alexandria, VA: Association for Religious and Value Issues in Counseling.

Callahan, D. (1988). The role of emotion in ethical decision making. *Hastings Center Report, 18*(3), 9–14.

Carroll, M., Schneider, H., & Wesley, G. (1985). *Ethics in the practice of psychology*. Englewood Cliffs, NJ: Prentice Hall.

Casas, J. M., Ponterotto, J. D., & Gutierrez, J. M. (1986). An ethical indictment of counseling research and training: The cross-cultural perspective. *Journal of Counseling and Development, 64*(5), 347–349.

Cayleff, S. E. (1986). Ethical issues in counseling, gender, race, and culturally distinct groups. *Journal of Counseling and Development, 64*(5), 341–344.

Christiansen, H. D. (1972). *Ethics in counseling: Problem situations.* Tucson: University of Arizona Press.

Cochrane, D. (1979). Prolegomena to moral education. In D. Cochrane, C. Hamm, and A. Kazepides (Eds.), *The domain of moral education* (pp. 73–88). New York: Paulist Press.

Cohen, B. (1975/1976). Principles and situations: The liberal dilemma and moral education. *Proceedings of the Aristotelian Society* (New Series), *76*, 75–87.

Corey, G., Corey, M. S., & Callanan, P. (1993). *Issues and ethics in the helping professions.* Pacific Grove, CA: Brooks/Cole.

Corey, G., Corey, M. S., & Jackson, J. V. (1990). The role of group leader's values in group counseling. *Journal for Specialists in Group Work, 15*(2), 68–74.

Daniluk, J. C., & Haverkamp, B. E. (1993). Ethical issues in counseling adult survivors of incest. *Journal of Counseling and Development, 72*(1), 16–22.

Dienhart, J. W. (1982). *A cognitive approach to the ethics of counseling psychology.* Washington, DC: University Press of America.

Dillon, R. S. (1992). Respect and care: Toward moral integration. *Canadian Journal of Philosophy, 22*(1), 105–132.

Downey, R. S., & Telfer, E. (1969). *Respect for persons.* London: Allen & Unwin.

Drane, J. F. (1982). Ethics and psychotherapy: A philosophical perspective. In M. Rosenbaum (Ed.), *Ethics and values in psychotherapy: A guidebook* (pp. 15–50). New York: Free Press.

Elliott, C. (1992). Where ethics come from and what to do about it. *Hastings Center Report, 22*(4), 28–35.

Farley, M. A. (1993). A feminist version of respect for persons. *Journal of Feminist Studies in Religion, 9*(Spring/Fall), 183–198.

Fischer, L., & Sorenson, G. (1985). *School law for counselors, psychologists and social workers.* New York: Longman.

Frankena, W. K. (1973). *Ethics.* Englewood Cliffs, NJ: Prentice Hall.

Frankena, W. K. (1986). The ethics of respect for persons. *Philosophical Topics, 14*(2), 149–167.

Frazier, D. M. (1980). The interaction between ethical standards of counsellors and their legal responsibility. *Canadian Counsellor, 14*(4), 235–241.

Gaus, G. (1989). Practical reason and moral persons. *Ethics, 100*(1), 127–148.

Green, T. (1960). *The activities of teaching.* New York: McGraw-Hill.

Gustafson, K. E., & McNamara, J. R. (1987). Confidentiality with minor clients: Issues and guidelines for therapists. *Professional Psychology: Research and Practice, 18*(5), 503–508.

Hare, R. M. (1972). *Applications of moral philosophy.* Berkeley: University of California Press.

Hare, R. M. (1981). The philosophical basis of psychiatric ethics. In S. Block & P. Chodoff (Eds.), *Psychiatric ethics.* Oxford: Oxford University Press.

Hare-Mustin, R. T., Marecek, J., Kaplan, A. G., & Liss-Levinson, N. (1979). Rights of clients, responsibilities of therapists. *American Psychologist, 34*(1), 3–16.

Hass, L., & Malouf, J. (1988). Personal and professional characteristics as factors in psychologists' ethical decision making. *Professional Psychology: Research and Practice, 19*(1), 35–42.

Hass, L., Malouf, J., & Mayerson, N. (1986). Ethical dilemmas in psychological practice: Results of a national survey. *Professional Psychology: Research and Practice, 17*(4), 35–42.

Herlihy, B., & Golden, L. (1990). *Ethical standards casebook.* Alexandria, VA: American Association for Counseling and Development.

Hoffman, J. C. (1979). *Ethical confrontation in counseling.* Chicago: University of Chicago Press.

Houts, A. C. (1986). Can religion drive you crazy? Impact of client and therapist religious values on clinical judgments. *Journal of Consulting and Clinical Psychology, 54*(2), 267–271.

Hume, D. (1957). *An inquiry concerning the principles of morals* (C. W. Hendel, Ed.). Indianapolis, IN: Bobbs-Merrill.

Hummel, D. L., Talbutt, L. C., & Alexander, M. D. (1985). *Law and ethics in counseling.* New York: Van Nostrand Reinhold.

Huxley, A. (1955). *Brave new world.* Harmondsworth, U.K.: Penguin Books.

Ibrahim, F. A. (1986). Ethical standards for cross-cultural counseling: Counselor preparation, practice, assessment, and research. *Journal of Counseling and Development, 64*(5), 349–351.

Ivey, A. E., & Rigazio-DiGilio, S. A. (1992). Counseling and psychotherapy as moral and spiritual practice: Facing a major paradigm shift. *Counseling and Values, 37*(1), 39–46.

Kant, I. (1956a). *Critique of practical reason* (L. Beck, Trans.). Indianapolis, IN: Bobbs-Merrill.

Kant, I. (1956b). *Groundwork of the metaphysics of morals* (3rd ed.) (H. J. Paton, Trans.). New York: Harper & Row.

Kant, I. (1963). *Lectures on ethics* (L. Infield, Trans.). New York: Harper & Row.

Kaufman, M. (1991). Post-*Tarasoff* legal developments and the mental health literature. *Bulletin of the Menninger Clinic, 55*(3), 308–322.

Keith-Spiegel, P. (1977). Violation of ethical principles due to ignorance or poor professional judgment versus willful neglect. *Professional Psychology, 8*(3), 288–296.

Keith-Spiegel, P., & Koocher, G. P. (1985). *Ethics in psychology: Professional standards and cases.* New York: Random House.

Kelly, M. (Ed.) (1988). *An ethical standards casebook* (Canadian Guidance and Counseling Association). Scarborough, ON: Nelson Canada.

Kermani, E. J., & Drob, S. L. (1987). Tarasoff decision: A decade later—dilemma still faces psychotherapists. *American Journal of Psychotherapy, 41*(2), 271–285.

Kitchener, K. S. (1984). Intuition, critical evaluation, and ethical principles: The foundation for ethical decisions in counseling psychology. *Counseling Psychologist, 12*(3), 43–55.

Kitchener, K. S. (1985). Ethical principles and ethical decisions in students affairs. *New Directions for Student Services, 30*(June), 17–29.

Kitchener, K. S. (1986). Teaching applied ethics in counselor education: An integration of psychological processes and philosophical analysis. *Journal of Counseling and Development, 64*(5), 306–310.

Koocher, G. P., & Keith-Spiegel, P. C. (1990). *Children, ethics, and the law: Professional issues and cases.* Lincoln: University of Nebraska Press.

Kopels, S., & Kagle, J. D. (1993). Do social workers have a duty to warn? *Social Service Review, 67*(1), 101–126.

Levenson, J. L. (1986). When a colleague practices unethically: Guidelines for intervention. *Journal of Counseling and Development, 64*(5), 315–317.

London, P. (1986). *The modes and morals of psychotherapy* (2nd ed.). New York: Norton.

Lowe, C. M. (1976). *Value orientations in counseling and psychotherapy* (2nd ed.). Cranston, RI: Carroll Press.

MacLagan, W. (1960). Respect for persons as a moral principle (Pt. 1). *Philosophy, 35*(134), 193–217.

Mappes, D. C. (1985). Conflict between ethics and law in counseling and psychotherapy. *Journal of Counseling and Development, 64*(4), 246–252.

Maslow, A. (1968). *Toward a psychology of being.* Princeton, NJ: Van Nostrand.

Maslow, A. (1970). *Motivation and personality.* New York: Harper & Row.

Mill, J. S. (1956). *On liberty.* Indianapolis, IN: Bobbs-Merrill.

Mill, J. S. (1971). *Utilitarianism* (Samuel Gorovitz, Ed.). Indianapolis, IN: Bobbs-Merrill.

Mills, M. J., Sullivan, G., & Eth, S. (1987). Protecting third parties: A decade after *Tarasoff. American Journal of Psychiatry, 144*(1), 68–74.

Monahan, J. (1993). Limiting therapist exposure to Tarasoff liability: Guidelines for risk containment. *American Psychologist, 48*(3), 242–250.

Moore, G. E. (1994). *Principia ethica.* New York: Cambridge University Press.

Newmark, C. S., & Hutchins, T. C. (1981). Survey of professional education in ethics in clinical psychology internship programs. *Journal of Clinical Psychology, 37*(3), 681–683.

Nyberg, D. (1991). The basis of respect is caring. *Proceedings of the Philosophy of Education Society, 47,* 197–201.

Olson, R. G. (1967). Deontological ethics. In P. Edwards (Ed.), *Encyclopedia of Philosophy* (Vol. 2, p. 343). New York: Macmillan.

Owen, G. (1986). Ethics of intervention for change. *Australian Psychologist, 21*(2), 211–218.

Parr, G. D., & Ostrovsky, M. (1991). The role of moral development in deciding how to counsel children and adolescents. *School Counselor, 39*(1), 14–19.

Patton, M. J., & Meara, N. M. (1992). *Psychoanalytic counseling.* New York: Wiley.

Pelsma, D. M. (1986). Experience-based ethics: A developmental model of learning ethical reasoning. *Journal of Counseling and Development, 64*(5), 311–314.

Peters, R. S. (1960). Freud's theory of moral development in relation to that of Piaget. *British Journal of Educational Psychology, 30*(3), 250–258.

Peters, R. S. (1970). *Ethics and education.* London: George Allen & Unwin.

Pettit, P. (1989). Consequentialism and respect for persons. *Ethics, 100*(1), 116–126.

Plato. (1991). *The republic of Plato* (2nd ed.) (A. Bloom, Ed.). New York: Basic Books.

Pope, K. S., & Vasquez, M. J. T. (1991). *Ethics and psychotherapy and counseling: A practical guide for psychologists.* San Francisco: Jossey-Bass.

Powell, C. J. (1984). Ethical principles and issues of competence in counseling adolescents. *Counseling Psychologist, 12*(3/4), 57–68.

Rawls, J. (1971). *A theory of justice.* Cambridge, MA: Belknap Press of Harvard University Press.

Rest, J. R. (1984). Research on moral development: Implications for training counseling psychologists. *Counseling Psychologist, 12*(3/4), 19–29.

Rich, J. M. (1984). *Professional ethics in education.* Springfield, IL: Charles C. Thomas.

Richards, N. (1978). Using people. *Mind, 87*(345), 98–104.

Robinson, S. E., & Gross, D. R. (1989). Applied ethics and the mental health counselor. *Journal of Mental Health Counseling, 11*(3), 289–299.

Rogers, C. R. (1961). *On becoming a person: A therapist's view of psychotherapy.* Boston: Houghton Mifflin.

Rogers, C. R. (1980). *A way of being.* Boston: Houghton Mifflin.

Rousseau, J. J. (1974). *Emile* (B. Foxley, Trans.). New York: Dutton.

Rudinow, J. (1978). Manipulation. *Ethics, 88*(4), 338–347.

Russell, B. A. W. (1935). *Religion and science.* New York: Henry Holt.

Russell, B. A. W. (1955). *Human society in ethics and politics.* New York: Simon & Schuster.

Schulte, J. (1990). The morality of influencing in counseling. *Counseling and Values, 34*(2), 103–108.

Sherrer, C. W. (1980). *Ethical and professional standards for academic psychologists and counselors.* Springfield, IL: Charles C. Thomas.

Smart, J. J. C. (1967). Utilitarianism. In P. Edwards (Ed.), *Encyclopedia of Philosophy* (Vol. 8, pp. 206–212). New York: Macmillan.

Smith, J. L. (1993). Report of the ACA [American Counseling Association] Ethics Committee: 1992–1993. *Journal of Counseling and Development, 72*(2), 220–222.

Spellman, E. V. (1978). On treating persons as persons. *Ethics, 88*(2), 150–161.

Steere, J. (1984). *Ethics in clinical psychology.* Cape Town, South Africa: Oxford University Press.

Stein, R. H. (1990). *Ethical issues in counseling.* Buffalo, NY: Prometheus Books.

Strike, K. (1982). *Liberty and learning.* New York: St. Martin's Press.

Strike, K., Haller, E., & Soltis, J. (1988). *The ethics of school administration.* New York: Teachers College Press.

Strike, K., & Soltis, J. (1985). *The ethics of teaching.* New York: Teachers College Press.

Szasz, T. (1974). *The myth of mental illness.* New York: Harper & Row.

Tarasoff v. Regents of the University of California, 529 P. 2d 553 (Cal. 1974); 551 P. 2d 334, 331 (Cal. 1976).

Toulmin, S. (1981). The tyranny of principles. *Hastings Center Report, 11*(6), 31–39.

Van Hoose, W. H., & Kottler, J. A. (1977). *Ethical and legal issues in counseling and psychotherapy.* San Francisco: Jossey-Bass.

Van Hoose, W. H., & Paradise, L. V. (1979). *Ethics and counseling in psychotherapy: Perspectives in issues and decision making.* Cranston, RI: Carroll Press.

Waldo, S. L., & Malley, P. (1992). Tarasoff and its progeny: Implications for the school counselor. *School Counselor, 40*(1), 46–54.

Weil, M., & Sanchez, E. (1983). The impact of the Tarasoff decision on clinical social work practice. *Social Service Review, 57*(1), 112–124.

Welfel, E. R. (1992). Psychologists as ethics educator: Successes, failures, and unanswered questions. *Professional Psychology: Research and Practice, 23*(3), 182–189.

Welfel, E. R., & Lipsitz, N. E. (1983). Moral reasoning of counselors: Its relationship to level of training and counseling experience. *Counseling and Values, 27*(4), 194–203.

Welfel, E. R., Lipsitz, N. E., Neal, E., & Jackson, J. V. (1984). The ethical behavior of professional psychologists: A critical analysis of the research. *Counseling Psychologist, 12*(3/4), 31–42.

Wilson, L. S. (1993). The state of ethical training for counseling psychology doctoral students. *Counseling Psychologist, 15*(3), 334–341.

Wollstonecraft, M. (1891). *A vindication of the rights of woman, with strictures on political and moral subjects.* London: T. Fisher Unwin.

Worthington, E. L. (1988). Understanding the values of religious clients: A model and its application to counseling. *Journal of Counseling Psychology, 35*(2), 166–174.

Wulsin, L. R., Bursztajin, H., & Gutheil, T. G. (1983). Unexpected clinical features of the Tarasoff decision: The therapeutic alliance and the "duty to warn." *American Journal of Psychiatry, 140*(5), 601–603.

Zahner, C. J., & McDavis, R. J. (1980). Moral development of professionals and paraprofessionals, counselors, and trainees. *Counselor Education and Supervision, 19*(4), 243–251.

Index

About the Authors

John M. Schulte has a broad range of experiences in public schools as a teacher, principal, and supervisor of student teachers. He received his Ph.D. degree in Philosophy of Education from the University of Wisconsin and has been a member of the Department of Social and Philosophical Foundations of Education at California State University, Northridge since 1964. He is currently Professor Emeritus at that institution. Throughout his career, he has maintained an interest in moral philosophy and ethics and has worked closely with school counselors in the field to identify and analyze ethical problems and issues.

Donald B. Cochrane is a professor of education at the University of Saskatchewan. Most of his research and writing focuses on ethical aspects of education. He is co-editor of *The Domain of Moral Education* (1979), *The Development of Moral Reasoning: Practical Approaches* (1980), *Philosophy of Education: Canadian Perspectives* (1982), and the editor of *So Much for the Mind: A Case Study in Provincial Curriculum Development* (1988). He has been the Associate Editor of *Moral Education Forum* since its inception nearly 20 years ago.